CALIFORNIA EDUCATION:

A Brief History

Irving G. Hendrick

series editors:
Norris Hundley, jr.
John A. Schutz

Boyd & Fraser Publishing Company
San Francisco

CALIFORNIA EDUCATION:
A BRIEF HISTORY

Irving G. Hendrick

© copyright 1980 by Boyd & Fraser Publishing Company, 3627 Sacramento Street, San Francisco, CA 94118. All rights reserved.

Manufactured in the United States of America.

Library of Congress catalog card number: 80-80027

ISBN 0-87835-097-7

1 2 3 4 5 · 4 3 2 1 0

EDITORS' INTRODUCTION

MENTION THE NAME CALIFORNIA and the popular mind conjures up images of romance and adventure of the sort that prompted the Spaniards in the 1540s to name the locale after a legendary Amazon queen. State of mind no less than geographic entity, California has become a popular image of a wonderful land of easy wealth, better health, pleasant living, and unlimited opportunities. While this has been true for some, for others it has been a land of disillusionment, and for too many it has become a place of crowded cities, congested roadways, smog, noise, racial unrest, and other problems. Still, the romantic image has persisted to make California the most populated state in the Union and the home of more newcomers each year than came during the first three hundred years following discovery by Europeans.

For most of its history California has been shrouded in mystery, better known for its terrain than for its settlers—first the Indians who arrived at least 11,000 years ago and then the Spaniards who followed in 1769. Spaniards, Mexicans, and blacks added only slightly to the non-Indian population until the American conquest of 1846 ushered in an era of unparalleled growth. With the discovery of gold, the building of the transcontinental railroad, and the development of crops and cities, people in massive numbers from all parts of the world began to inhabit the region. Thus California became a land of newcomers where a rich mixture of cultures pervades.

Fact and fiction are intertwined so well into the state's traditions and folklore that they are sometimes difficult to separate. But close scrutiny reveals that the people of California have made many solid contributions in land and water use, conservation of resources, politics, education, transportation, labor organization, literature, architectural styles, and learning to live with people of different cultural and ethnic heritages. These contributions, as well as those instances when Californians performed less admirably, are woven into the design of the Golden

State Series. The volumes in the Series are meant to be suggestive rather than exhaustive, interpretive rather than definitive. They invite the general public, the student, the scholar, and the teacher to read them not only for digested materials from a wide range of recent scholarship, but also for some new insights and ways of perceiving old problems. The Series, we trust, will be only the beginning of each reader's inquiry into the past of a state rich in historical excitement and significant in its impact on the nation.

Norris Hundley, jr.
John A. Schutz

CONTENTS

INTRODUCTION

I N REFLECTING ON the history of education in California, one cannot help but be awed by the developments of the last century and a quarter. From modest beginnings the educational system has grown into an enterprise consisting of nearly five million students in about ten thousand public and private schools and colleges, and all sustained by an annual budget well in excess of five billion dollars. Its massive size immediately inspires questions about its development and purposes.

The fate of education early became linked with the fate of public schooling. Prior to the mid–nineteenth century the public's educational concerns were limited largely to the practical need for acquiring literacy. Relatively little attention was given to whether such training should be supported with public or private funds. By the time California entered the Union, however, the public school already had become the nation's dominant educational institution. Private schooling was never eliminated; indeed its continuance seemed essential for maintaining the principle of free choice in America. Yet as important as private endeavor was to remain, it was soon dwarfed by the public school, an institution that by the seventh decade of the last century embraced as its mission not only instruction in basic subjects, but an almost evangelical commitment to historic democratic purposes.

A half century ago historians of education regarded the public schools as among the finest manifestations of democracy, the "great equalizer of human condition," to borrow a phrase made famous by Horace Mann, the nation's most prominent nineteenth-century apostle of public schooling. More recent scholars see public schooling as only one among many educative forces in American culture, and some view it as a "miseducative" force. Among the latter are those who see education as social control, as a racist, class-based system, which has served the needs of the white middle class, but which has neglected, even harmed, the poor and the nonwhite.

On balance, public education in California has not assured equality of opportunity for all citizens, but neither has it been a disaster perpetuated by cynical, calculating officials, bent only on enhancing the interests of a ruling elite. The expansion of schooling opened new doors of opportunity for the masses while also helping to preserve political and cultural traditions. The public's investment in education has paid handsome dividends for individuals and for society as a whole. The California experience, however, suggests that those dividends rarely have been distributed equally and have often been determined by race, location of housing, and family traditions. Finding the basis of equality has not been easy for Californians, who have resisted busing their children to distant schools and moving teachers to schools around their cities. They point to their schoolhouses and colleges as the best equipped in the nation and to the history of education since 1769 as a remarkable story of achievement.

CHAPTER ONE

Education under Spanish and Mexican Governments

LONG BEFORE SPANISH explorers claimed California for the crown, Indians engaged in word-of-mouth instruction. Through oral tradition and informal apprenticeship, Indian youth became proficient hunters and homemakers, and in turn passed these skills along to their children. Until the founding of missions after 1769, Spain's claim to California in 1542 made no practical difference to the native population. Even then most of the approximately 300,000 native Californians remained untouched by the Spanish and Catholic influence.

Though Spain's direct control of California lasted a mere half-century, the establishment of twenty-one missions represented a major educational achievement. Each mission offered religious instruction as well as vocational training necessary for the survival of the Spanish colonial enterprise in California. Receiving emphasis were the industrial arts, including instruction in carpentry and farming, for boys; and cooking, sewing, and homemaking for girls. The Third Council of Lima in 1583 had also obligated church officials to teach Indians in their native dialects, but this goal suffered from enormous practical difficulties. Rarely did all Indians at a particular mission speak the same idiom. Contrary to Spanish hopes, Christian Indians brought by the padres from Baja California were unable to acquire the native idioms rapidly and easily. As happened occasionally, when the padres failed to take seriously their charge to teach Indians in their native tongue, they were admonished by the comisario-prefecto to reform their negligent ways.

Aside from the education of Indians at the missions, a few intermittent efforts were made to provide formal schools during the Spanish period. Diego de Borica, the seventh Spanish governor of Alta California (1794–1800), did attempt to initiate schools for young Spaniards, but with no recorded successes.

Hardly had Mexico assumed control over California in 1822 than a determined effort began to secularize the missions. Agitation for secularization had predated Mexican independence by more than a decade, but was not implemented until ordered by Mexican authorities in the late 1820s and early 1830s. In a practical sense, secularization effectively ended the educational program of the missions, as mission property slipped rapidly into private hands. The contribution of Mexico to institutionalized education was seldom tangible but reflected noble intentions and plans. Mexican authorities were faced with enormous difficulties. They were limited by a small population of loyal citizens, approximately eight thousand in 1846; by substantial financial restraints; and by communication and transportation difficulties between the federal capital in Mexico City and the provincial capital in Monterey, and between the provincial capital and scattered small towns. These problems meant that few schools were established during the Mexican period, 1822–1846.

Still, several Mexican governors hardly can be faulted for lack of effort in education. In response to the implorings of Governor José María Echeandía for priests to provide for the secular training of the Indians, Father Narciso Durán of Mission San Jose complained in 1841 that he could not even find ignorant schoolmasters for the white race, let alone do anything more than provide practical education for Indians. Governor José Figueroa exhorted local leaders and parents—both Indian and non-Indian—to improve the existing schools in Monterey, Santa Barbara, and Los Angeles and to establish new ones in Sonoma,

Santa Clara, San Jose, San Gabriel, San Luis Rey, and San Diego. He founded a state-supported school at San Gabriel for the training of teachers and directed each town to send its most promising Indian and white students to the institution. In the 1830s Figueroa encouraged the learned Englishman William E. P. Hartnell, who had married into a Mexican family, to establish the only secondary school during the Mexican period, El Colegio de San José. Opened in January 1834, the school enrolled a mere fourteen students and managed to survive only a year and a half. Although it featured practical subjects as well as the modern languages, philosophy, and theology, El Colegio de San José simply did not have an adequate population base from which to draw its enrollment.

Later governors, especially Juan Bautista Alvarado and Pío Pico, appeared no less interested in supporting good schools than Figueroa had been. Alvarado experienced some limited success in recruiting teachers from Mexico, but was plagued by lack of funds to pay their salaries. Pico, the last Mexican governor of California, recommended that teachers be paid from the public purse and that schools be organized whenever and wherever sufficient numbers justified them. He even went so far as to propose compulsory attendance of children in schools, but his bright hopes were dashed by a major shift in the political fortunes of California. Even had Mexico retained control of the region, the sparse Mexican population probably could not have been reached by a state system of education.

CHAPTER TWO

Beginnings of a Yankee School System

DURING THE EARLY 1840s an ever increasing number of newcomers from the United States took up residence in California. By 1846 this group had grown to nearly seven hundred persons in a total non-Indian population of approximately eight thousand.[1] With the Americans came Yankee values emphasizing education, including a concern for mass literacy, civility, and moral behavior as interpreted by the Protestant faith. The newcomers also brought with them their collective experience with social institutions, including a high regard for the state system of schooling—a system available to all children, at least all white children, and supported by public taxation. Public schools, they believed, should be free from sectarian direction, and they acknowledged that local control of schools could be limited, at least partially, by the creation of state boards of education and by state legislative influence over the curriculum. Except for a relatively few elite private academies and proprietary schools, most of which were located in the eastern states, private control of education already had become identified with the Catholic Irish and Germans who wanted to protect themselves from Protestant influences.

As early as 1847 Sam Brannan, a transplanted New Yorker and publisher of San Francisco's *California Star,* argued forcefully for the erection of public schools. His effort won community support and led, in February 1848, to the election of a five-member school board in San Francisco. Public funds were set aside for the erection of a suitable structure and the partial payment of a teacher's salary. Although the school operated partially on public funds, the boys and girls who attended were charged tuition. Thomas Douglass, a graduate of Yale College, became the school's first teacher. Noble values of teaching and learning notwithstanding, Douglass and many of his students soon heard the call of gold and left for the diggings. Over the next few years similar sporadic efforts at keeping school were initiated in San Francisco, Los Angeles, and Santa Barbara.

Of greater long-term importance to public schooling was the action taken by delegates assembled at Colton Hall, Monterey, in September 1849, to draft California's first constitution. Surprisingly little discussion greeted presentation of Article IX, section 1, providing for the election of a superintendent of public instruction; this section was approved, though the idea was by no means common. Only four states—Michigan, Iowa, Wisconsin, and Vermont—had previously provided for an elected chief school officer through the constitutional process.

Section 2 of the same article involved money, and that proved to be a more troublesome topic. Central to the controversy was a desire by some delegates to allow funds derived from the sale or rental of public lands to be used for purposes other than education. Since adoption of the Northwest ordinances of 1785 and 1787, new states entering the Union had received federal lands for the support of schools. Approximately 500,000 acres had been given to California by the federal government. While tradition was on the side of devoting all funds derived from land sales to the schools, Sacramento attorney Winfield S. Sherwood argued that some of the acres might be located on gold mines, thus becoming too rich a source to be devoted exclusively to education. After spirited debate and exhortations about education being the foundation of the republic, Sherwood's proviso was defeated by a vote of 18 to 17. Adopted without debate was another section calling for the founding of a state university.

A key achievement of the Monterey convention was the

creation of a framework for a common school system operated by local townships under the supervision of an elected state superintendent of public instruction. Legislation approved in 1851 and 1852, during the administrations of John G. Marvin, California's first superintendent of public instruction, and his successor, Paul K. Hubbs, apportioned school funds among the several towns and cities "in proportion to the number of children residing therein between the ages of 5 and 18." The 1852 law also called for a state school tax of five cents on each $100 of assessed valuation of property. In addition, incorporated towns and counties were permitted to levy a school tax of not more than three cents. A year later counties were authorized— but not required— to raise by taxation any amount they desired for school purposes. The system was not yet being supported adequately, but it was becoming increasingly clear that public schools were to be operated at public expense.

The first city to take advantage of the state public school laws was San Francisco, California's major urban center. In September 1851, the city council enacted a Free School Ordinance providing for the establishment, regulation, and support of free common schools. The structure and powers of the first local school board are still recognizable today. The ordinance created a board of education that was linked to the city government by having as members one alderman and one assistant alderman plus two citizen members. Powers of the board included authority to appoint a superintendent of schools, purchase property, build schools, prescribe a course of study, hire teachers, and inspect the schools twice or more each year. Then, as now, the superintendent served as executive officer of the board with responsibility for carrying out the board's orders and managing the school system. In the absence of state standards for teacher certification, he was also responsible for selecting and certifying teachers.

Demands for schooling in San Francisco during the early 1850s were greater than the new system could accommodate. By the fall of 1853, 1,399 pupils had enrolled, and a year later the number had grown to 1,745. Had ample facilities been available, the board projected that 2,500 of the 2,730 children of school age could have been enrolled.[2]

San Francisco's lead was quickly followed by smaller towns.

Perhaps the greatest stimulus to the establishment of schools was the high value placed on formal education by those who had experienced its benefits. Communities often built school houses before other public buildings. By January 1854 Californians were supporting 47 common schools, in which 4,052 pupils attended classes for at least three months a year.[3] Most of the schools were ungraded, and problems in finding qualified teachers, adequate facilities, and sufficient revenue frequently limited sessions to six months or less. Still, progress was remarkable, the more so since the state did not require local communities to establish schools.

Through the 1850s California's state school superintendents exhorted members of the legislature to support the schools generously, but with minimal success. Three fundamental issues have characterized the debate over financing for public education. The first two involved the source and amount of funding, while the third concerned the distribution of those funds. In the early years of statehood revenue obtained from the sale of public lands helped support the schools, but it was seldom adequate to the task. Taxation could raise the needed funds, but usually not without stiff opposition from the community. While many legislators maintained that it was in society's interest to provide for public schools, some objected to spending public funds for the education of other people's children. In a message to the legislature in 1855, State Superintendent Paul Hubbs complained bitterly about the legislature's inactivity, and accused the lawmakers of being responsible for the "immoral tendencies of trained ignorance in our land." "No government is worthy of the name of civilization," he asserted, "that refuses to educate, and to educate properly, the children of the state."[4] Three-fourths of the children in California, Hubbs claimed, were growing up unable to read or write.

Rhetorical pleadings with the legislature notwithstanding, substantial improvements in supporting public education were not realized until the mid-1850s when Andrew J. Moulder became California's third state superintendent of public instruction and quickly made his views felt. He was bright and experienced, having finished college at the age of sixteen and worked successively as a tutor, teacher, and professor in Virginia. Outspoken in his opinions, he brought to the state superintendency a greater comprehension of school procedures and policies than did any of his predecessors. More articulate too, he advocated a system of free schooling as well as racial segregation.

Much of Superintendent Moulder's argument for the instruction of children at public expense appeared to be rooted in his desire to preserve the established social order. If effective means were not taken to improve the schools, he warned in his 1858 annual report, the state would soon be in the hands of "benighted men and women." The legislature, he complained, had recently "paid nearly three times as much for the support of four hundred criminals as for the training and culture of thirty thousand children."[5] By the time he left office in 1862, Moulder had persuaded the legislature to implement Article IX, section 2, of the constitution by establishing a state school fund from proceeds of public land sales (1861) and to create a state normal school for the training of teachers (1862).

Less ennobling was Moulder's inclination to play on the racial fears of legislators. Key among his successful recommendations to the legislature in 1858 was a bill prohibiting local school districts from admitting persons of "inferior races," especially blacks, to schools attended by whites. Democrats of Moulder's stripe were generally harsher in their attitude toward blacks than were Republicans loyal to the ideology of Abraham Lincoln. Moulder lashed out against the "Negrophilist school of mock philanthropists" who had found their way into California. "In several of the counties," he complained, "attempts have been made to introduce children of Negroes into our public schools on an equality with whites." The danger, as Moulder saw it, was the dreaded prospect of amalgamation:

> Until our people are prepared for practical amalgamation, which will probably not be before the millennium, they will rather forego the benefits of our schools than permit their daughters— fifteen, sixteen, and seventeen years of age plus— to affiliate with the sons of Negroes. It is practically reduced to this, then, that our schools must be maintained exclusively for whites, or they will soon become tenanted by blacks alone.[6]

In the same report Moulder urged the legislature to withhold funds from any district "that permits the admission of the inferior races— African, Mongolian, or Indian— into the Common Schools." Lest anyone suspect his motives, the state superintendent disclaimed prejudice "against a respectable Negro—in his place." The legislature granted Moulder's request to deny state school funds to erring districts, and it approved his recommendation that local trustees be empowered to use public funds to support separate schools for nonwhites. In a sense, Moulder's cause focused more on closing a loophole than on implementing a new policy. As early as 1855 the legislature had mandated that state school funds be distributed in proportion to the number of white children in each school.

While Andrew J. Moulder made solid contributions as state school superintendent, his successor, John Swett, was the most notable and is the best remembered, ranking in American history with Horace Mann of Massachusetts, Henry Barnard of Connecticut and Rhode Island, Calvin Wiley of North Carolina, and John Pierce of Michigan. The son of a New England schoolmaster, Swett had gone to California in 1853 and soon became principal of the Rincon school in San Francisco. His articulate and vigorous campaign for improved schools during the next decade helped win him the Union party's nomination for state superintendent and his election in 1862.

Swett differed from his predecessors in the state superintendency in terms of outlook, vigor, and political effectiveness. From his public statements and actions it is clear that he genuinely subscribed to the ideal of extending free school opportunities to blacks as well as whites. Whereas Moulder had grudgingly agreed with this orientation on the grounds of fairness, Swett was committed to it. But even Swett's democratic tendencies were compromised by the political realities of the times as he pursued vigorously his objective of providing free schools for as many children as possible.

In spite of constitutional provisions for education and some enabling legislation during the 1850s, the state had not yet moved decisively toward an extensive system of free public schooling. During 1862, his final year in office, Superintendent Moulder had complained that the state's contribution to public school support was "a pittance almost beneath contempt."[7] More successfully than his predecessors, Swett was able to persuade the legislature and the public generally of their obligation to bring public schools under centralized state control and sustain them with substantive state and local support. Even at that, until 1870 public schools were permitted to exact fees from parents in proportion to the number of children they sent to school. These "rate bills," as they were known, served to supplement the funding provided by the state and local school districts. The schools laws of 1864 and 1866 did much to make rate bills unnecessary and stand as the major products of Swett's persuasion.

In his biennial report of 1865 Swett addressed the issue of a tax on real property, a concept that was resisted initially by many laborers as well as by wealthy citizens and business interests. "Public schools are synonymous with taxation," Swett maintained, "and the sooner the common people understand this democratic-republican doctrine, the better for the state, the better for property, the better for mankind, the better for the nation."[8] Happily for him, a key provision of the 1864 act was a requirement that all proceeds from the annual state tax of five cents on each one hundred dollars of taxable property be applied to teachers' salaries. Equally important was a requirement that each county levy an annual tax sufficient to raise at least two dollars for each school child between the ages of four and eighteen. Prior to this legislation no minimum county tax rate had been fixed in law. Rarely did county supervisors avail themselves of earlier tax provisions which were merely permissive in character.

Swett's ultimate legislative victory came in the 1866 session, and it was that victory more than any other that earned him his place in history. Several important advances for the cause of free schools were contained in an omnibus school bill entitled "An Act to Provide for a System of Common Schools." In financial terms the act increased the funding authorized in 1864 by levying a state tax of 8 cents on each $100 of taxable property and permitting the counties to spend an additional amount of $3 per child on education so long as the maximum tax required to attain that level did not exceed 35 cents on each $100 of real property. The act also required each school district to furnish to children at public expense all school supplies except textbooks, ordered school trustees to levy a district tax sufficient to keep schools open five months a year, and provided for the establishment of separate schools for nonwhite children.

John Swett, Superintendent of Public Instruction, 1863–1867. (*Photograph [circa 1865] courtesy of the Bancroft Library, University of California, Berkeley.*)

The full extent of Swett's victory cannot be appreciated without an awareness of his extensive lobbying activity. Being well aware that an economy move was under way in the legislature in 1865, Swett mounted a large-scale public relations campaign to convince lawmakers that free public schools were vital to the welfare of California. He appealed to legislators to keep in mind that a liberal expenditure for schools was in the end the truest form of economy. Schools, after all, educated and shaped the character of men and women who would become the producers of society's wealth and participants in its government.

On the likely chance that legislators would not reach these conclusions on their own, Swett organized a massive petition campaign and other strategies to persuade them. Petitions numbering into the tens and twenties arrived daily on the desks of legislators during the 1866 legislative session. Working closely with the Assembly and Senate Education committees— even to the extent of serving without additional compensation as the secretary to both committees— Swett mounted such an awesome campaign on behalf of free schools that most legislators quickly joined his cause. Politically Swett had the advantage of drawing substantial support from the rural areas of the state. Only San Francisco stood to contribute more in taxes than the city would derive in benefits. Not unexpectedly, it was there that the opposition was centered.

So impressive had been Swett's leadership that he drew favorable comment from educators around the nation. The famous eastern school leader Henry Barnard devoted ten pages in his *American Journal of Education* to the new California school law and praised Swett's work as a "noble contribution to the interests of national education, which laid our whole country under lasting obligation."[9]

As the 1866-1867 school year ended, Swett claimed with pride that California common schools were, for the first time, "made entirely free for every child to enter."[10] Actually his claim was exaggerated in one important respect. The new legislation permitted a local school board, by majority vote, to admit into schools for whites "half-breed Indian children and Indian children who live with white families or under the guardianship of white persons."[11] Other nonwhites would be allowed to attend school with whites only if a school district could not provide for their instruction in any other way, and only if the policy was approved by a majority vote of the local trustees. Even then, a majority of white parents could reverse the policy.

This legislation was merely the latest in a series of discriminatory practices, some sanctioned by law and others by custom. Relief was obtained only through the courts or through the disadvantaged group's persistence and power. Policies of exclusion, later of separation, and finally of desegregation resulted from a shifting collage of attitudes and circumstances. Through it all a basic American commitment to fairness competed with racist attitudes for primacy in the policy maker's mind. In the end, both were generally compromised in favor of various pragmatic forces.

By the time John Swett left office in 1867, the state's school system was enrolling approximately forty-six percent of California's white children and forty percent of its black children, but fewer than one percent of the Indian and Asian children were attending classes. The near absence of schooling for these children may be explained by white prejudice and their own cultural orientation which contrasted dramatically with that of the dominant white society. Moreover, in the case of Indians, few schools were located near their homes.

For those students—mostly whites—who attended school, great variation existed in the quality of instruction and facilities. In the spring of 1865 Swett toured the state, visiting schools in Los Angeles, San Gabriel, Wilmington, San Bernardino, Santa Barbara, and San Jose, among others. While generally pleased with the efforts of teachers and students, he lamented the physical facilities. The students' desks in Los Angeles, he observed, were "admirably adjusted to twist the spines of growing girls, and break the backs and weary the legs of the sturdier boys." At that they were preferable to the ones he found in San Bernardino: the "roughest, meanest, most rickety, broken-down-looking substitutes for seats which ever disgraced a school room."[12] Of the schools visited, only the one at Montecito could boast a library—and it was a small one.

Swett also expressed concern over teacher qualifications, pedagogical methods, and textbooks, some of which he was able to deal with effectively in the school legislation of 1866. Although most of the schools he visited in 1865 were ungraded single-room structures, within the next decade the eight-year graded school, imported from the eastern states, became the norm in California's larger cities. Whether graded or ungraded, the schools of the late nineteenth century emphasized the traditional values of patriotism, obedience, moral training, industry, and punctuality. Effort, authority, and discipline dominated the outlook of teachers, administrators, and school board members.

There were, to be sure, some newer pedagogical trends which were featured in the educational journals of the day. Most notable of these was the technique of "object teaching," which had been developed by the Swiss educator Johann Heinrich Pestalozzi and implemented in Oswego, New York, by Edward A. Sheldon during the early 1860s. Object teaching stressed the importance of learning through direct acquaintance with the actual object of knowledge, thereby appealing to the student's senses. Teaching through observation and the use of pictures received a notable boost from the Pestalozzians. Theoretically the role of books was to be diminished since the learning of words was presumed to follow from direct experience with the things to which the words referred. In actual practice textbooks remained the most important force in the curriculum, not only in the central subjects of reading and arithmetic, but in spelling, geography, grammar, and science as well. The modest qualifications of most teachers seemed to assure the primacy of textbooks.

The first two decades of statehood had witnessed substantial progress in the establishment of a constitutional framework for public schooling, and— by the 1860s— the actual organization and support of a state system of education. If schoolhouses, school furniture, and school equipment were often primitive, they were not noticeably worse than similar facilities found in villages and cities outside of California. Thanks to the work of such early educators as Moulder and Swett, teachers were regularly appraised of the latest pedagogical theories and were otherwise equipped to serve the state's children. Clearly much work remained, including the fundamental task of persuading more parents that schooling was vital to their children's future.

CHAPTER THREE

Extending the Reach of Public Education

THE MAJOR CONCERN of educators in the decade following John Swett's incumbency was extending the benefits of education to more children. With that objective in mind, the legislature approved in 1874 "An Act to Enforce the Educational Rights of Children." This measure required the attendance in school of children between the ages of 8 and 14 and set penalties for noncompliance. The new law reflected the national trend toward compulsory attendance and a measure of disappointment by school leaders that the famous school law of 1866 had not stimulated greater voluntary attendance. The 1874 legislation was aimed at those whom State Superintendent Henry Bolander identified as "that large class of people who, through self-interest, carelessness, or ignorance, ignore the claims of their children to the rights and benefits of at least a common school education."[1] Although California was among the first states to enact a compulsory attendance law, another half century passed before the popular mood supported a serious and vigorous effort to enforce it.

As important as getting children to school was what happened to them once they arrived. Prior to the widespread use of standardized aptitude and achievement tests after World War I, the most common means of assessing educational attainment was through the use of statistics on school attendance, years of schooling, and literacy. During the 1850s educators often commented on the illiteracy of California youth. With only the rarest exceptions, good education was equated with instruction in reading and writing and all manner of practical studies. Some exercises in spelling and punctuation were included, but the third "R," arithmetic, was seldom emphasized until late in the century. Nonacademic offerings, such as physical education, were ignored, albeit by the 1880s some time was devoted to a wide range of outdoor games.

The complaints of California educators and parents notwithstanding, the state fared well in the surveys of literacy conducted in the nineteenth century. For the white population ten years of age and older, the illiteracy rates were 7.0 percent in 1870, 4.4 percent in 1880, 4.5 percent in 1890, and 3.1 percent in 1900. While illiteracy was more widespread among blacks, the comparative figures were not dramatically different during the early years: 7.4 percent in 1870, 7.8 percent in 1880, 7.7 percent in 1890, and 13.4 percent in 1900. For Californians of both races, the illiteracy rates compared favorably to the nation at large. The national percentages for the white population ten years of age and over were 13.1 in 1870, 10.2 in 1880, 8.3 in 1890, and 6.6 in 1900.

California educators were generally eager to correct the illiteracy problems through compulsory school attendance. If the rhetoric of schoolmen can be believed, public school authorities and legislators probably valued the compulsory attendance policy more highly than did parents. Other governmental actions seem to have more closely reflected the public will. The second state constitutional convention of 1878–1879 is a case in point. About a third of the 152 delegates represented the highly vocal and reform-minded Workingmen's party, which was dominated by San Francisco labor leaders. A majority of delegates (98) represented the more traditional and conservative business and farming interests of the state.[2] Contrary to the fears of some state educators who worried about the influence of the Workingmen's party, the convention was not hostile to education. On the nine-member Education Committee were four lawyers, two physicians, one lumber dealer, one merchant, and a clerk. Most were college educated, and while some had been elected as "Nonpartisans," every man on the committee was a registered Republican. Happily for the state's school interests, the delegates were generally agreed on the major educational issues. They approved the provisions submitted by the Education Committee, and those provisions favored the democratization of the school system.

The State Board of Education was perceived by the public as a corrupt body, a reputation it earned primarily through its capricious administration of teacher examinations. Many citizens favored a shift in responsibility for public education from the state to the local level. Accordingly, the new constitution extended the term of elected county superintendents from two to four years, prohibited the legislature from passing laws dealing with the management of local public schools, granted authority to certify teachers to county superintendents, and most importantly, assigned the right to adopt textbooks—and thus control a large share of the curriculum—to local boards of education and country superintendents.

A key section, submitted by former State Superintendent John Swett, called for inclusion of high schools within the public school system. Some teachers resisted the move because they feared that populist sentiments among delegates would interpret the section as elitist. As a consequence, a teacher delegate added a proviso: "the entire revenue derived from the state school fund should be applied exclusively to the support of primary and grammar schools." The amended section was adopted as proposed, although Swett believed that the original section could have passed just as easily without the proviso.

Hardly had the constitution been ratified before the Workingmen's State Convention, meeting in San Francisco in June 1879, adopted a new forty-plank platform, number thirteen of which called for strengthening the state's weak compulsory attendance law, extending free school benefits to include secondary education through age fourteen, and providing free state-printed textbooks for all children.[3] By advocating free texts for all children, the Workingmen's party went at least one step beyond what the other major parties were advocating. At best the dominant view favored selling texts to parents and guardians at actual cost. Not until 1912 were free textbooks distributed to students.

The failure of supporters to win free textbooks for children in the early 1880s should not overshadow their victory on a related front. In 1883 Senator George H. Perry of San Francisco advocated a constitutional amendment requiring that California texts be authored by Californians and printed in the state printing office. Perry believed the amendment would aid the drive for free education and prevent textbook profits from flowing to eastern publishers. His amendment proved more attractive than the appeal of local control over the selection of texts. On election day in 1884, his proposal won the support of all major political parties, the labor unions, most legislators, and the parents who had been purchasing the textbooks. While the insistence on California authors soon proved impractical, state printing of texts endured for over eighty years.

The decision to provide low-cost textbooks occurred at a time of substantial expansion in school enrollments. Some of the increase merely reflected the growth in state population. In Los Angeles, school attendance shot up so rapidly during the 1880s that the city resorted to double sessions. With impressive growth came bonds to finance the construction and furnishing of school buildings. In 1887–1888, twenty-one bond elections and fifteen special tax elections won approval in Los Angeles County alone. One result of the rapid population growth in southern California during the eighties was the establishment of many small schools near new subdivisions. During the great land boom of the 1880s southern California parents valued the convenience and security of having small schools located close to their homes as well as the greater control over school policy which this situation permitted. School administrators were less enthusiastic because of the gross inefficiencies resulting from numerous small facilities.

By 1910 nearly 94 percent of California's 173,945 children between ten and fourteen years of age were attending school, as were 78 percent of the 139,639 chidren between the ages of six and nine. Among whites of native parentage, the percentages of attendance stood at 94.6 for the ten through fourteen age group, and 78.5 for the six through nine age group. In the case of blacks those percentages were 94.0 and 81.1, respectively. But while California's few black children were achieving parity with whites, at least in terms of passing through the schoolhouse doors, such was not the case with other nonwhites. In the six through nine age range, the attendance percentages dropped to 49.1 for Indians, 59.8 for Chinese, and 51.2 for Japanese.

That black children were being admitted to schools—and were attending them in respectable numbers—was the result of initiative and political skill exercised by black parents during the previous half century. As early as the 1850s, many educated black families in California were insisting that education held the greatest hope for the economic, social, and political progress of their race. By the 1870s and 1880s the principal focus of their political and legal action was on segregated schools.

In November 1871, black leaders launched their campaign against segregation by canvassing widely for funds and retaining a highly respected white attorney, John W. Dwinelle. In July 1872, several black parents attempted unsuccessfully to enroll their children in a "white" public school in San Francisco. Attorney Dwinelle selected the grievance of Harriet A. Ward, mother of Mary Frances Ward, as the most promising for building a legal challenge. Two months later he sought relief for the Ward family by applying for a writ of mandate from the California Supreme Court, alleging that the school principal had violated Mary Ward's rights under the Thirteenth and Fourteenth amendments to the federal Constitution by denying her admission to the school nearest her home. To the chagrin of Dwinelle, in February 1874 the court saw the matter differently. Chief Justice William T. Wallace, speaking for the court, wrote:

> ... in the circumstances that the races are separated in the public schools, there is certainly to be found no violation of the constitutional rights of the one race more than of the other, and we see none of either, for each, though separated from the others, is to be educated upon equal terms with that other, and both at the common public expense.[4]

Although this decision occurred twenty-two years prior to the U.S. Supreme Court's landmark acceptance of separate but equal facilities in the case of *Plessy* v. *Ferguson,* it was a clear pronouncement of that doctrine.

There was a silver lining in the decision. "Unless such separate schools be in fact maintained," the court insisted, "all children of the school district, whether white or colored, have an equal right to become pupils at any common school organized

under the laws of the State. . . ." Two months later the legislature ended the segregation of black and Indian children in
places where separate schools were not provided. In 1880 it
forbade segregation of blacks, even in those communities which
had taken the trouble to provide separate schools. The action
was made easier by the relatively modest number of blacks in
most communities and by the financial burden of maintaining
separate schools. In 1880 the state's total black population as
reported in the U.S. Census was 6,018, while according to the
state superintendent of public instruction, the number of black
children between the ages of five and seventeen in school
was 802.

Untouched by the new legislation was any change in the
segregationist policy toward a much more concentrated population of Chinese children. The latter were served to a limited
extent beginning in the 1870s by several small private Chinese
language schools operating in San Francisco. Like similar schools
that served other immigrant groups, the Chinese schools held as
their primary goal the preservation of the native language and
culture, a goal far different then from the mission of public
education.[5] Children of minority groups often attended schools
in the late afternoons or on Saturdays in order to get the
language instruction their parents regarded as essential.

Equality of educational opportunity was far from a reality.
Still, opportunities for public schooling had been extended ap-
preciably during the last quarter of the nineteenth century and
with that extension had come expected gains in literacy. Educators, though somewhat suspicious and fearful of the populist
rhetoric advanced by leaders of the Workingmen's party, soon
found that their fears were largely unwarranted. Furthermore,
not all educational progress was attributable to the efforts of
educators. Populist initiative was responsible for making state-
printed textbooks available to pupils at low cost. Similarly, the
initiative of black parents had produced an end to the legal
segregation of their children in public schools. But despite that
particular advance in equality, the century ended in a social
climate that generally supported extended public school opportunities for whites and severely limited opportunities for nonwhites.

CHAPTER FOUR

Expansion and Discrimination at the Turn of the Century

A T THE TURN OF THE CENTURY California was still over-whelmingly agricultural in social and economic outlook, but political and educational leaders realized that the increasing urbanization and industrialization required a system of mass education that extended beyond mere literacy. Not everyone was expected to benefit from such an extension, however, and it was only through hard-fought efforts that nonwhites were able to enjoy public schooling at any level. With a few notable exceptions, the educational and economic disparities between whites and nonwhites became more acute, as did tension and conflict between the two groups. Exclusion from school and segregated schooling produced disadvantages even in nineteenth-century society, but those disadvantages worsened significantly in the more complex and urbanized society of the twentieth century.

On the occasion of his inauguration as governor in 1903, George Pardee complained that Californians were not taking sufficient advantage of public schooling. He had a point. In

1900 California ranked thirteenth among the states in percentage of children between five and eighteen years of age enrolled in school.[1] Though the ranking was modest, the percentage of school enrollments was still much higher than it had been forty years earlier. City schools now boasted superior facilities, adequately qualified teachers, and the most up-to-date educational resources. Even so, general statewide changes did not appear dramatic. Organized schooling in San Francisco and Los Angeles was becoming formal and systematized, but in other places the pattern of neighborhood control prevailed. One new development of major importance was the rise of public high schools.

Already by 1900 high schools were viewed nationally and in California as absolute requirements for the new industrial age. Breakthroughs in the sciences, coupled with the application of scientific discoveries to commercial and domestic technologies, suggested that more than mere literacy would be necessary to meet the requirements of employment and effective citizenship. Still uncommon in 1900, high schools received their legal basis of support in California between 1886 and 1902.

An 1895 amendment to the state High School Act of 1893 permitted any city or incorporated town having a population of a thousand or more to establish a high school district. The constitutional amendment of 1902, while requiring that all revenue derived from the state school fund and school tax be applied to the support of primary and grammar schools, also authorized the legislature to levy a special tax for the support of high schools and technical schools. With state financing, beginning in 1904, came dramatic enrollment increases in grades nine through twelve, a fact that is vividly reflected in U.S. Census reports: enrollments increased from 12,620 in 1900, to 39,650 in 1910, and to 126,913 by 1920.

The extension of schooling from eight to twelve grades during the first half of the twentieth century also provided opportunities to reorganize the structure of the educational system. Additional enrollment reflected more than growth in the population; it reflected a broadening of the schools' reach to include the children of working-class parents. With additional numbers came a wider range of student abilities and career goals. In the end, however, economic incentive as much as pedagogic stimulation led to the reorganization of secondary schooling.

In the 1909–1910 school year occurred the first example of reorganization when a junior high school was established in Berkeley. City Superintendent Frank F. Bunker and the local board of education were impressed by the need to provide additional room for incoming ninth grade pupils at the high school. Financial constraints made it impractical to enlarge the school, but Bunker found the needed space by rearranging the traditional grouping of pupils.[2] In place of the usual elementary and high schools, he established the high school proper, comprising the tenth, eleventh, and twelfth grades; an introductory high school (soon to be known as the junior high), comprising the seventh, eighth, and ninth years; and an elementary school, comprising all children of the first six grades. Besides alleviating the space problem, Bunker also sought to increase the attractiveness of education for that substantial group of pupils who had been dropping out at the end of the fifth grade. He hoped the new arrangement would encourage the children of working-class families to remain in school at least one year longer than they had been doing.

In spite of the attractiveness of a system that paralleled the physical, intellectual, and social development of children, junior high schools grew slowly in number. Not until the mid-1930s did they become common, and even then they were absent from many communities until the late 1940s. Eventually, however, both the junior high school and the two-year intermediate school (which covered only the seventh and eighth grades) became widespread. Rarely was the choice of organization based exclusively, or even primarily, on educational considerations. Often it was determined by the kind of school districts found in a particular area.

Unified districts, those responsible for education in grades kindergarten through twelve, generally established the three-year junior high schools. Elementary districts, those concerned only with grades kindergarten through eight, could select either the traditional kindergarten through grade eight arrangement, or incorporate the newer junior high school or two-year intermediate school. Children living in elementary districts were inevitably also served by a larger union high school district having responsibility for grades nine through twelve.

The last decade of the nineteenth century and the first two decades of the twentieth century witnessed elements of both the old and the new in educational racial policies as well as in the arrangement of grades. With the legal segregation of blacks in California ending in 1880, and their widespread resegregation still awaiting the growth of cities, the most prominent racial policies of the period affected Asians.

Of all the long-standing discriminatory educational policies implemented between passage of the Chinese Exclusion Act of 1882 and the Japanese and Korean Exclusion Act of 1924, the most publicized was an attempt in 1906 to segregate Japanese children in the public schools of San Francisco. In May of the previous year the city's school board went on record favoring such a course. Their action was based on the alleged evil consequences of having white children—especially young girls—associate with those "of the Mongolian race." They were also reacting to crowded conditions which, it was argued, had allowed "many" Japanese pupils to enroll to the exclusion of "our children."[3]

In September 1906 the city reestablished its Chinese primary school at 926 Clay Street as the "Oriental School" and assigned a principal and four teachers to it. Other city principals were then directed to send their Chinese, Japanese, and Korean students to the school. Affected by the order were ninety-three Japanese, including twenty-two second-generation Japanese Americans who were native-born citizens of the United States (Nisei).

The segregation of students was not a novel step. Chinese children had been segregated in San Francisco for nearly half a century. Thousands of other nonwhite children, mainly Indians, were being denied even segregated schooling. What was exceptional about the 1906 segregation order in San Francisco was the blatant political motivation of the action and its international repercussions. Mayor Eugene Schmitz, the most prominent advocate of segregation, had been reelected in 1905 on a platform advocating separate schools for Asians. One day before the segregation order was issued, Schmitz was indicted on graft charges. It is likely that the indictment made it necessary for

him to rally popular support and deflect as much adverse pub-
licity as he could.

President Theodore Roosevelt's personal interest in the issue,
dictated by its foreign-policy implications, held promise for
securing a reversal of the segregation order. A strongly worded
protest from the Japanese government prompted Roosevelt to
dispatch Secretary of Commerce and Labor Victor H. Metcalf
to San Francisco to investigate what the president termed a
"wicked absurdity." In December, Metcalf reported that he
could find no justification for the segregation policy.

Both Japanese officials and San Francisco school authorities
were prepared to argue the issue in the courts, but Roosevelt
sought a quick solution. He invited the entire San Francisco
school board (accompanied by the mayor whose invitation came
from the board) to Washington in February 1907.[4] After a week
of discussion, the federal administration offered to check the
influx of Japanese immigrants in exchange for a promise from
San Francisco officials to repeal the segregation order. The
school incident ended, but agitation for exclusion of Japanese
and restrictions on their ownership of land continued in California for more than a decade.

While the experience of Japanese students in San Francisco
illustrates how racial antipathy could compromise the democra-
tizing values of public education, the long-term disadvantages
experienced by the Japanese were less apparent than those felt
by most other nonwhite minorities. Even though discriminated
against, the Japanese commitment to American education remained strong during the era, thereby permitting pupils from
that culture to maximize the benefits they received from schooling. Unlike the interest shown in racial segregation by many
contemporary social scientists, educators, and jurists, most educators of those early years in the century simply were uncon-
cerned by the likely effects of school segregation. Other matters
received their attention, particularly the expansion and reorganization of schooling and a host of educational innovations produced by social and intellectual forces.

CHAPTER FIVE

Changing Pedagogical Ideologies and Practices

SEVERAL SOCIETAL FORCES profoundly altered the nature of California education during and after World War I. Urbanization and population growth continued to have an impact, as did the war itself. The draft and recruiting program for the war effort revealed large numbers of illiterates and individuals in poor physical condition. The state and nation responded quickly. In 1917 California added physical education to the curriculum and two years later increased the compulsory school attendance age to sixteen. With the Smith-Hughes Act of 1917 Congress offered the states financial assistance for vocational education. An increased sensitivity to national values during the war gave a substantial boost to courses in U.S. history, Americanization, and citizenship. On the negative side was a wave of superpatriotism which led the California Board of Education and similar boards elsewhere in the nation to suspend the teaching of the German language in public high schools.

Of greater long-term impact than the war was the increasing urbanization of society, coupled with steady growth in the population. These changes were accompanied by an increase in the power of professional educators at the expense of local boards of education, which acted more and more on the advice of professionally trained superintendents. The progressive period in California politics during the early 1900s appeared to return power to the people through the establishment of the initiative, referendum, and recall, but less so in the formulation of policies for the school system. Revulsion against partisan politics in school board affairs prompted voters to turn out Workingmen and to replace them with allegedly "nonpartisan," local businessmen. In the process, parents lost some influence in the education of their children, but teachers gained greater job security and independence from undue community intervention than they had enjoyed earlier.

Accompanying these developments, and in a sense stimulating them, was the rapid growth of school enrollment beginning with World War I. Both public and private schools shared in the growth, although there was never any doubt about the dominance of public institutions. Several sponsors of Protestant parochial schools, most notably the Missouri Synod of the Lutheran Church and the Seventh Day Adventists, accelerated their development of schools after the war. Their efforts were dwarfed, however, by those of the Roman Catholics. The dominant Protestant character of American society—including public schools—provided Catholics with a special incentive for maintaining their own school system. Church policy in America, as expressed in the First Plenary Council of Baltimore in 1852 and the *Code of Canon Law* (1918), left little doubt that separate schools were much preferred for Catholic children. Until the 1960s millions of dollars were spent on opening new school facilities, especially district high schools in the Los Angeles area. Nevertheless, the church's lack of financial resources necessitated the attendance of numerous Catholic youth in public schools.[1]

Even with an accelerating effort at founding private schools, the private school share of total enrollment remained very small, well under ten percent of the state total. By 1920 the state superintendent of public instruction could report that enrollment in public elementary schools stood at 500,644, an 11.6 percent increase over 1918. Enrollment in public secondary schools reached 162,832 in 1920, an increase of 28.3 percent over 1918.[2]

With such an upturn in enrollment came a marked increase in the complexity of school administration and its impact upon the office of the state superintendent. Edward Hyatt, the incumbent during this wartime period, was known for his simple, unhurried manner and attentiveness to rural teachers, an administrative style that was out of step with the rapidly changing era. Greatly weakened by illness, Hyatt in 1918 was defeated in his bid for reelection by Will C. Wood, a man who had served the State Board of Education for five years as commissioner of secondary schools. Though not a college graduate, Wood was effective in dealing with urban constituencies and large staffs of employees. Prestigious though the state superintendency became among school people, it did not hold Wood who in 1927 left the office to become state banking commissioner. Capable administrators could earn better salaries in business, or even as superintendents of large city school districts.

During his eight-year tenure, Wood expanded the administrative role of his office and supported successfully several important school bills, with provisions that required school districts to file their budgets annually with the state superintendent, prohibited county boards of supervisors from cutting school district budgets, granted tenure to teachers, and established a new credential in the supervision and administration of schools. Because schools were (and still are) under the control of numerous bodies— the legislature, the state board of education, and county or local district boards— it was important for the state superintendent to have sufficient authority to act decisively in enforcing state school laws and regulations of the state board. Likely the most important educational changes of a legal nature to occur in California during the 1920s resulted from Proposition 16, a multifaceted amendment to the state constitution which passed by an overwhelming vote in 1920. The amendment added kindergartens to the state school system, established teachers' colleges to replace the two-year normal schools, provided for a stronger base of state and county school support, and required all state aid, plus sixty percent of country funds supporting local school districts, to be used for teachers' salaries.

While these developments held special long-range significance for the schools, the financial provisions were especially important to local school boards and administrators who were responsible for the educational programs in their districts. To be sure, other important financial plans had been adopted over the years, including a major amendment to the constitution which eliminated the state property tax in 1910. While this earlier amendment had given the public school system and University of California first claim on state revenue, it had not determined the amount of state support guaranteed to the schools. Proposition 16 corrected that oversight by mandating an annual minimum state contribution of $30 per pupil in grades one through twelve. Counties were obligated to raise revenues sufficient to match that amount for elementary schools and double it for high schools. Average daily attendance (ADA), as counted in the previous year, became the standard for school apportionments. With a realistic minimum amount of state funding guaranteed, the schools were able to weather economic crises, including the depression of the 1930s.

Generally unrelated to the specifics of school finance, but still reflecting larger social and economic forces, was the curriculum reform movement known as "progressive education." Even before World War I San Francisco State Normal School, led by President Frederic Burk, had become a center of educational reform. Recitations and daily assignments were abandoned at San Francisco State's demonstration school in favor of individualized instructional programs. Students progressed at their own rates, being tested and advanced as soon as their work was completed. One of America's more notable early private progressive schools, the Ojai Valley School, was founded by Chicago pump manufacturer Edward Yeomans in 1923. Yeomans, a member of the Winnetka, Illinois, school board during the 1920s, had become closely identified with the progressive education movement through his association with Carleton Washburne, Winnetka superintendent and a former professor of education at San Francisco State. Yeomans' book, *Shackled Youth,* published in 1921, was highly critical of the alleged "academic lockstep" in public schools.[3]

An element of notoriety for the Ojai Valley School aside, California's principal contribution to the progressive education

Helen Heffernan, Director of the Division of Elementary Education and Rural Schools, State Department of Education, 1925-1965. (*Photograph* [*circa* 1945] *courtesy of Dr. William Davis, Archivist, State of California.*)

movement was in the public sector. In 1925 Helen Heffernan began disseminating the progressive gospel in rural and urban schools alike. For nearly forty years she served as director of the Division of Elementary Education within the California State Department of Education. A graduate of the University of California, Berkeley (A.B., 1924, M.A., 1925), she probably did more to implement the progressive doctrine than any educator in the nation. That doctrine held that the school curriculum should reflect the needs and interests of society and the individual; indeed, the school was perceived as a miniature community. Major tenets of the theory had been defined by the American philosopher John Dewey at the turn of the century, and were most actively proclaimed during the 1920s and 1930s by the faculty at Teachers College, Columbia University, in New York.

While Teachers College became the ideological center of the progressive movement, no state demonstrated greater enthusiasm for implementing progressive verities than California. Faced with the task of educating vast numbers of youth, California educators turned for direction to the scientism of the day, primarily psychology and the new testing movement. Even among educators there were some differences in emphasis. Most high school teachers and administrators, while accepting the desirability of broadening the curriculum in order to accommodate a wider range of students, remained essentially subject-matter oriented.

Other educators, primarily those working in elementary schools, tended toward a child-centered focus, with their primary and overriding emphasis on the social and emotional needs of the child. Those needs, presumably having been determined by careful study, would be considered in producing a curriculum leading the student toward personal growth and social adjustment as well as imparting knowledge likely to prove useful in coping with life's challenges. For progressives of all stripes, new and experimental procedures of instruction were equated with strength (goodness), old or traditional methods with weakness (evil).

Many of California's elementary educators remained faithful to progressive principles through the 1930s and 1940s and into the 1950s. "We are endeavoring," wrote Lorraine Sherer, Los Angeles County's curriculum director in 1932, "to guide thoughtful teachers to a complete acceptance of the Dewey philosophy."[4] With Helen Heffernan directing the curriculum reform effort in Sacramento, and several of her protégés occupying key administrative positions in county school offices, most of the newer trends in education received enthusiastic acceptance in California. Of these trends, the most popular was the transformation of the primary school so that all activities were centered around the child's immediate environment and diagnosed needs— social, psychological, and physical.

In addition to a well organized state plan for disseminating the progressive gospel in the schools, some local systems initiated programs of their own. The Los Angeles city schools constituted the largest progressive system in the nation, or, at the very least, the most "progressive" large system in the nation. In 1924 Los Angeles became the first California city to adopt an activity program for grades kindergarten through six.[5] Consistent with current pedagogical thinking, the activity program included field trips, role-playing experiences, and various student projects, all intended to build upon the interests and pre-

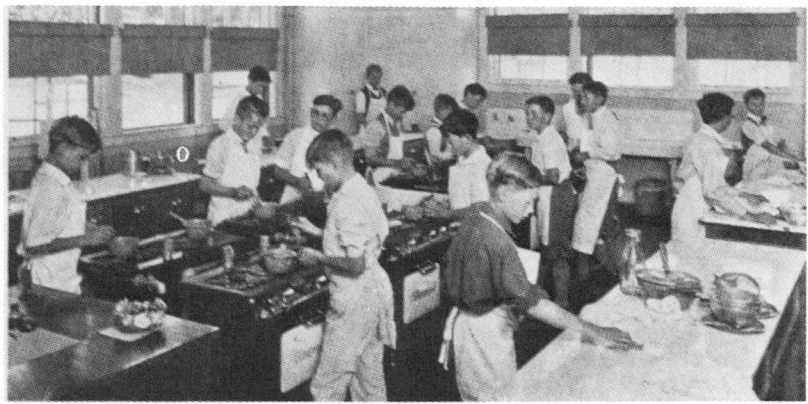

"Boys Too Are Interested in Cooking": Gardner Street School, Los Angeles.
(*Photograph appeared originally in* Progressive Education, VIII [*October* 1931],
p. 485.)

vious learning of students. All parts of the curriculum, as well as
instructional methods, were subject to modification in order to
accommodate differences among pupils.

To the extent that the new progressive philosophy was embodied in the work of a single elementary school during the
1930s and 1940s, that school was University Elementary School,
a laboratory facility administered by the University of California, Los Angeles. Corinne Seeds, UES's energetic director,
was rivaled only by Helen Heffernan as the most influential
elementary educator in California. Often working in close association with Heffernan and other progressives, Seeds and her
colleagues at UES influenced numerous teachers who toured the
school and took summer training courses and county training
institutes.

While secondary schooling was also touched by progressive
theory, that influence was muted. In general, university en-
trance requirements served to restrain progressive forces on the
secondary level. A theoretical case was made for combining
certain subjects, most frequently English and "social studies,"
and for making traditional courses more relevant to solving
present-day problems. But there were other more practical
forces at work as well. The law required that certain subjects be
included in the curriculum— for example, manners and morals,

An uppergrade rendition of a pioneer dance, Bryant School, Long Beach, California. (*Photo appeared originally in* Progressive Education, xv [*January* 1938], *p.* 48.)

dangers of alcohol and narcotics, fire prevention, American history and civics, public safety and accident prevention. Nothing in the law indicated how the subjects should be taught. Pedagogical theory aside, a constantly expanding legislated curriculum, coupled with a finite number of hours in the school day, seemed to require that some broadly inclusive courses be formed. "Social studies," emphasizing history, but including geography, economics, sociology, and other subjects, became a course commonly adopted to cope with both theoretical and practical pressures on the curriculum.

Nothing characterized the national influence of progressives on secondary schooling more than the Eight-Year Study (1932–1940) conducted by the Progressive Education Association. The association sought to show that success in college was not dependent on a single pattern of course work. It began by selecting a highly diverse group of thirty public and private schools of differing size. For a period of five years, beginning in 1936, the schools agreed to recommend their graduates to cooperating colleges without regard to course and unit requirements. Of the thirty schools, two were in California—Eagle Rock High School in Los Angeles and University High School in Oakland. The findings of the study, published in 1942, indi-

"Arithmetic in Action: Computing the Growth of Wheat." (*Los Angeles County Schools, Visional Education Division. Photograph appeared originally in* Progressive Education, XVII [*February* 1940], *p.* 91.)

cated that students in the progressive schools performed at least as well academically and socially in college as students with similar backgrounds who had attended traditional schools. Indeed, graduates of schools that varied most widely from the traditional pattern performed better than graduates from those schools that varied least.[6]

Although results from the Eight-Year Study were promising, one cannot infer with assurance that the progressive influence either strengthened or weakened the cause of pupil learning. Assessing the success of a particular trend in education is complicated by such variables as the conditions of a child's home life, child-rearing practices, and teacher skills. At least in the short run, most progressive school systems appeared satisfied with their programs. In 1939 Los Angeles school officials reported that student achievement was generally higher than it had been in 1924 or in 1937.[7]

Ironically, it was San Francisco school administrators who received the brunt of criticism for progressive practices. Unlike their Los Angeles counterparts, they never officially endorsed progressive tenets, but they gradually adopted many progressive programs. In the spring of 1944, after hearing criticism for more than a year from citizens who believed the schools were

"Activities related to the economic and social life of the community are valuable at all age levels." (*Los Angeles County Schools, Visual Education Division. Photograph appeared originally in* Progressive Education, XVII [*February* 1940], *p.* 105.)

emphasizing "fads and frills," the San Francisco Board of Education solicited opinions concerning the schools' effectiveness from some 60,000 parents.[8] Although the questionnaire elicited many critical responses, over eighty percent of the parents believed that the schools were meeting the needs of their children. Still, the public was never as infatuated with progressive school practices as were the educators, though it was not until the 1960s that the public became alarmed about the relationship between progressive theory and the achievement—or lack of achievement—of their children.

Among the several faces of progressive education, perhaps the most colorful and controversial was "social reconstruction," a theory that had little to do with pedagogy but much to do with the relationship between social policy and the schools. Spawned by the despair of economic depression, the movement gained its identity from the speeches and writings of George C. Counts, a professor of education at Teachers College, Columbia University. In his famous 1932 essay, "Dare Progressive Education Be Progressive," Counts urged teachers to work for change in the nation's economy, transforming it from a system serving powerful and wealthy interests to one responsive to the needs of the poor.[9] Conditions were sufficiently desperate in 1932 and 1933 for his ideas to receive some serious consideration by educators, even those who were otherwise quite conservative.

By spring 1933, California State Superintendent of Public Instruction Vierling Kersey was defending President Franklin D. Roosevelt's policies for economic recovery as "not the end of our social order," but "the end of the weak and faulty in that social order." "Excessive profit must be prevented," counseled the state superintendent, "in order that the power to consume may be more widely distributed among all who participate in production." Later that same year he asserted that "we can accomplish by social reconstruction that recognition of social and economic equality for which many nations have found it necessary to undergo internal strife and revolution."[19]

Under earlier economic conditions Kersey had not avowed such ideas. His politically conservative credentials were perfectly in order. As a Republican, a Mason, a member of the Optimist Club, a life member of the Sons of the Revolution, he had regularly denounced dictatorships, fascism, anarchy, and communism, but the depression's impact caused him and other educators to doubt the viability of the American economic system.

Still, the infatuation of educators with social reconstructionist theory was short-lived. As early as 1935 the legislature, fearful of Communist doctrine spreading in the schools, mandated a loyalty oath for public school teachers. By 1947 the legislature's preoccupation with the emerging Cold War between the United States and Soviet Union led it to prohibit the use of state money for the purchase of materials associated with the "Building America" school magazine series. Since 1935 "Building America" had grown into the most popular of the curriculum series with a social reconstructionist orientation. Sponsored by the National Education Association's Society for Curriculum Study, the magazine provided teachers with information on such contemporary subjects as housing, transportation, commerce, and energy. In spite of impressive testimony to the contrary, the legislature concluded that the series smacked of subversive or Communist influence.

The legislature's ban on "Building America" was not so much a commentary on progressive education or social reconstructionist theory as a reflection of the national preoccupation with communism. The climate was abetted by sensational exposés in 1949 and 1950 of Alger Hiss, Whittaker Chambers, Judith Coplon, and others. Nationally, the mood of searching out Communists was personified by the activities of Senator Joseph R. McCarthy of Wisconsin and Congressman Richard M. Nixon of California. Local school boards were also affected. In 1951 the Pasadena board of education fired Willard Goslin, its super-intendent of schools, for allegedly aiding and abetting the twin bogies of progressive education and communism.[11]

On the state level Senator Jack B. Tenney of Los Angeles led the work of California's own Committee on Un-American Ac-tivities. Among Tenney's legislative proposals in 1949 was Sen-ate Constitutional Amendment 13, which would transfer from the University of California regents to the legislature the power to determine the loyalty of university employees. While SCA 13 received virtually no support in the legislature, it helped stimu-late the regents, in March 1949, to enact their own loyalty oath which they required all faculty members to sign. The oath's threat to freedom of inquiry and dissent prompted most faculty to denounce the measure, but eventually all but thirty-one com-plied with the requirement to sign. In August 1950, the non-signers were dismissed, not a one of whom was actually sus-pected of being a Communist, or even of being in sympathy with any suspected organization. Within months the regents' oath was superseded by a state oath, required by the Levering Act, applicable to all state employees.[12]

In compliance with a writ of mandate issued in 1952 by the California Supreme Court, the regents reappointed the non-signers who wished to return, if they signed the new state oath. That oath was eventually found unconstitutional by the state supreme court in 1967. Fortunately, the loyalty oath contro-versy did not ruin the careers of faculty who were young enough to resume their work. Many left the university and resumed productive careers elsewhere. Of those who returned, David S. Saxon, an assistant professor of physics at UCLA and the only assistant professor on the Los Angeles campus who had been dismissed, rose to become president of the university in 1975.[13]

The loyalty oath controversy, like the controversy surround-ing social reconstructionist curriculum materials before it, was an illustration of how public educational institutions can be affected by popular fears and prejudices. A more constructive lesson from the historical record is that schools often respond quite rapidly to social forces— albeit with varying degrees of success— by modifying their curricula and otherwise attempting to meet student needs.

CHAPTER SIX

The Professionalization of Teaching

DURING THE EARLY DECADES of statehood teachers enjoyed a closeness to their pupils and communities which they gradually lost under the press of industrialization and urbanization. The only qualification for teaching in those years was a willingness to teach and an ability to pass the scrutiny of a local school committee. Rarely were teachers required to possess a college education. An obvious consequence of minimal preparation and easy access was lost status and little independence in the management of schools.

No formal teacher training or certification requirements existed during the 1850s, although State Superintendent Paul K. Hubbs did organize teacher conventions in 1854 and in 1856 for the purpose of informing and inspiring teachers. In 1861 State Superintendent Andrew Moulder attracted 250 teachers to a three-day State Teachers Institute dedicated to enhancing their pedagogical skills. Featured topics at the event included a speech stressing the need for uniform state textbooks, a gymnastics demonstration, a discussion of school discipline, and a lecture on "Methods of Teaching." Similar events were held in 1862 and 1863.

Modest attempts to initiate teacher training and certification requirements occurred during the 1850s and 1860s. Both Andrew Moulder and John Swett persuaded the legislature to establish a state board of examiners to license teachers (1859) and a state normal school to train them (1862). Even after 1859 the testing and licensing of teachers followed no set pattern. Earlier responsibility rested with local districts. Then in the 1860s and early 1870s the state exercised control only to have that authority temporarily diluted under the state's second constitution, approved in 1879. Generally speaking, from the 1860s forward, the counties had authority to issue certificates to elementary teachers, an authority that was expanded under the second constitution to include "grammar-grade" (secondary) certificates as well.

Teachers gained status as a result of being certified. Indeed, their teaching credentials were coveted enough to stimulate cheating by others on state and county examinations. Questions on the state teachers' examination leaked out of Sacramento on one notorious occasion and created a major scandal. On Friday, November 29, 1878, the San Francisco *Evening Bulletin* printed the questions that were to appear on the examination scheduled for the following day. The city editor of the *Evening Bulletin,* posing as a teacher, had successfully secured the questions, thereby exposing corruption in the state's certification system. The scandal gave delegates to the second constitutional convention added incentive for placing the examination of teachers and the granting of certificates under local control.

The county examinations authorized in the second constitution for testing teacher fitness were hardly more successful—or less corrupt—than the state examinations had been. Much of the educational literature of the period reflected a growing dissatisfaction with the local system. In June 1887 the state board of education urged county board members to abstain from coaching candidates so that they passed the examinations. Little attention was paid to this request, and two years later the legislature made it a misdemeanor for a board member to prepare candidates.[1]

Greater state control over certification came after 1893 when the legislature empowered the state board of education to issue grammar-grade certificates and life diplomas to normal-school graduates.[2] The trend was reinforced in 1897 when the state supreme court ruled in *Mitchell* v. *Winnek* that the legislature could prescribe the requirements for teacher certification. The issue had been in doubt because the constitution had given county superintendents and boards control over teachers' examinations and teaching certificates.[3] In effect the ruling opened the door to a strange dualistic pattern of teacher licensure. Counties were still permitted to issue certificates, but all regularly licensed teachers were required to possess a state "credential" before the county could issue a "certificate." Except for a few emergency, substitute, and other short-term teaching authorizations that required only a certificate, the county certification process involved little more than registering state credentials.

State licensure requirements gave teachers two critical elements in their quest for professional status— acknowledgment that they possessed specialized knowledge and skills, and recognition in the law. Standards were not high, but they existed. Teachers, however, still had to convince the public— and themselves— that their specialized knowledge and skills were deserving of respectable salaries.

Leading the campaign for better salaries and teachers were persons who had left classroom teaching for positions in school administration. Their campaign was waged primarily through professional educational organizations. Between 1863 and 1875 the California Educational Society dominated the scene, though it was more concerned with publishing a journal to enhance the skills of teachers and securing more state funding for public schools than in advancing the status and working conditions of teachers. In June 1875 the society transformed itself into the California Teachers Association (CTA), but the name change reflected no real difference in direction. Key concerns remained the need for greater state support of public education, free textbooks for children, improved training of teachers, compulsory attendance, and expanded opportunities for manual training in the schools.

In 1902 the CTA became the second state educational organization in the nation to adopt a code of ethics. Drafted by the now venerable John Swett, the code defined unprofessional conduct for teachers, a key point being that competency alone should determine who acquired and retained teaching positions. Actually the requirement was aimed less at teachers than at administrators and board members who not infrequently had allowed friendships and politics to determine who received teaching positions.

After the turn of the century the CTA became more concerned with better salaries and retirement benefits for teachers. In 1910 it urged the legislature to establish a statewide teachers' pension system and a tenure plan. Both proposals were approved by the legislature in 1911, but the pension bill failed to win Governor Hiram W. Johnson's signature. Two years later the governor was persuaded to sign a similar bill.[4] CTA leadership also urged better salaries, arguing that good salaries would attract talented teachers and thereby help improve the quality of education. However, not until the 1930s, when the gravity of economic conditions forced attention on salaries, did compensation for teachers improve relative to the income of the population generally.

In 1916 events distant from California eventually became significant in the long-term campaign of teachers for greater autonomy and improved salaries. Eight teacher federations in the Midwest and East acquired charters from the American Federation of Labor and took the name of the American Federation of Teachers (AFT). The union's California affiliate, the California Federation of Teachers, was organized in 1919 and experienced roughly the same pattern of growth and decline as that of other unions—a decline during the 1920s and an increase during the depression years of the 1930s.

Though the AFT in time became the most vigorous advocate of the interests of classroom teachers, in its early years it was not a major force in educational policy. Union membership instilled fear among school board members, enough in fact for the San Francisco Board of Education to warn teachers in 1920 that union membership would cost them their jobs. Intimidation by local boards, discouragement by administrators, and weak organizational efforts combined to produce a decline in union membership during the 1920s. That notwithstanding, the national union movement of the 1920s attracted the most famous American educator, John Dewey. Although Dewey made no apology for the union's desire to improve the living standards of teachers, he focused his attention on the organization's programs for social reform. "I know of no organization except the American Federation of Teachers," said Dewey, "that stands constantly, openly, and aggressively for the realization of the social function of the profession."[5]

Dewey had a point. On the issue of equality for blacks, the AFT and its affiliate chapters in California had become about the only voice of educators demanding an end to school segregation and other forms of discrimination, but the union's principal focus was on the economic betterment of teachers and on greater teacher authority over students and the curriculum. Boards of education stood uniformly against the latter and also objected to surrendering authority over salaries to the collective-bargaining process. The CTA leadership, composed largely of administrators who viewed the association as a collegial body embracing all educators, also resisted greater teacher control over curriculum and instruction.

As a practical matter, the influence of the California Federation of Teachers (CFT) was modest outside of the largest cities before the 1970s, while the older CTA continued to represent most of the state's teachers. Prior to the 1960s the national union had not sought teacher allegiance. While accepting teacher members and occasionally offering them mild encouragement to join, the union did not campaign actively for membership.

Another factor helping to explain the CTA's supremacy was its emphasis on the need for a unified profession, which included not only teachers, but also administrators. Important as well, especially after World War II, was the rapid growth in population and strong support for schools, both occurring at a time when teachers were in short supply. If teachers' salaries were not high, at least they were on the rise, gaining steadily in relationship to the consumer price index throughout the 1960s.[6]

Even with improved salaries teacher organizations encountered major obstacles in their attempts to improve the status of their members. The general public was supportive of schools, but during the 1950s and 1960s critics of education claimed that American education had lost its vigor and strength. The critics' position was bolstered by the successful launching of the Soviet Union's Sputnik I, the world's first earth satellite, in the fall of 1957. Allegedly Americans were losing the "space race" because substantial knowledge rooted in the traditional disciplines was being subverted by too great an emphasis on classroom socialization, pedagogical tricks, and concern for learner "needs."

In 1961 the rhetorical assault transformed into a major legislative debate over teacher credential requirements. The result was the Fisher Act which mandated the elimination of college majors in education for future elementary teachers.[7] Instead, the new law required majors in academic subject-matter fields. Most faculty in schools of education, the CTA, and school administrators interpreted the Fisher Act as an attack by the legislature and Governor Edmund G. "Pat" Brown on the preparation of teachers. Nonetheless, they supported its mandate for a fifth year of college work for both elementary and secondary teachers.

The CFT, a group that identified more with subject-matter fields than with educational methodology, supported the bill. In spite of stormy controversy during the legislative debate, the teaching profession adjusted to changes produced by the Fisher Act. Although the education major was abolished, the Fisher Act did not limit the amount of course work in professional education that could be required in college and university teacher preparation programs. Ironically, in spite of heated debate over the Fisher Act in the 1960s, no evidence exists concerning the measure's long-term merits.

Hardly had the legislature changed certification requirements through the Fisher Act than it modified them again by passing the Ryan Act in 1970. That measure demonstrated the legislature's continuing determination to influence teacher preparation. The act increased the hours of student teaching needed for newly certified teachers, curtailed the number of courses in professional education that institutions could require prior to student teaching, and required state-supported teacher preparation institutions to make it possible for teacher candidates to finish their programs in four years. Faculty members in colleges and universities strongly objected. For the rest of the profession, especially teachers, the act contained a major affirmative feature, the creation of a Commission for Teacher Preparation and Licensing. The new commission represented a transfer in authority over teacher certification from the State Department of Education to a body representing all segments of the profession and public— teachers, university faculty members, school administrators, school services personnel (primarily counselors), school board members, and private citizens. Even though elementary and secondary teachers held but four of the fifteen seats on the commission, they had gained a greater voice in the formulation of teaching requirements than at any time in the state's history.[8]

Creation of a licensing commission did not automatically eliminate long-standing obstacles that had retarded teachers in their quest for professional status. The craft still lacked a sufficient body of hard scientific knowledge to establish itself as a profession. By limiting the number of theoretical courses required of students in schools of education, the Ryan Act reflected the view of critics that such courses were of modest usefulness. Also disturbing to the public and many educators was the lack of a successful system for updating periodically the knowledge and skills of teachers.

Many teachers, like the critics of their profession, were unconvinced that they possessed— or needed to possess— a special professional lore based on theory and scientific discovery. What mattered most in successful teaching, so it seemed, were a reasonable level of intelligence, good judgment, an undefined set of personality qualities, and practice teaching— and to many, these qualifications seemed hardly capable of eliciting "professional"— or higher— salaries from the public.

As public confidence in the schools and teachers began to wane in the late 1960s, the legislature became increasingly enamored with the idea that teachers should be held accountable for the performance of their students. The Stull Act, approved in 1971, sought to accomplish precisely that. Capitalizing on contemporary infatuation with a theory rooted in behavioral psychology, the "behavioral objectives movement," the Stull Act required teachers to define what they expected their pupils to learn. Local school boards were expected in turn to evaluate teachers on the extent to which the objectives were achieved. It quickly became apparent to virtually all concerned that the social and intellectual variables affecting pupil achievement made it impossible to implement such norms on the large-scale basis required by the Stull Act.

If teachers could not win professional deference from the public based on their special skills, they might at least be able to win gains through an appeal to fairness and by presenting a tougher public posture. In the 1960s collective bargaining became a topic of conversation among California teachers, and by the 1970s it had become a reality. As early as 1962 the United Federation of Teachers in New York City had called a strike, and in so doing had won the admiration and sympathy of teachers elsewhere in the country. In California the strike and related actions aided the organizational efforts of the California Federation of Teachers, especially in large cities.

By 1969 the Los Angeles Federation of Teachers had a membership of approximately 3,000. While still small in contrast to the California Teachers Association in Los Angeles, with its 19,200 members, the union gained strength in 1969 when it joined with its larger rival to form the United Teachers of Los Angeles, (UTLA), a body consisting of both CTA and CFT members. In May 1970 UTLA called a strike. Educational improvements and teachers' salaries were the issues. After five weeks the school board offered approximately $13 million for teacher salaries, announcing that the funds would come from money earmarked for educational improvements. The offer placed teachers in the difficult position of accepting the salary raise and watching educational programs deteriorate further, or continuing the strike and insisting on their original demands. In the end they did neither, voting 4,964 to 3,714 to end the strike and refuse the board's offer.[9] They won no tangible economic benefits, but claimed a moral victory for having called the community's attention to major problems in the school system.

Teacher strikes in New York, Los Angeles, and elsewhere demonstrated that city teachers were no longer satisfied with the cloak of professionalism at the expense of fair salaries and acceptable teaching conditions. The strikes also demonstrated that the AFT's activist-oriented collective-bargaining posture was better suited to the new attitude than the National Education Association's more passive "professional" approach, which stressed consultation between teachers and administrators. Taunted by the AFT as a "company union" and an "administrator dominated" organization, the NEA and its state affiliates, including the CTA, became militant themselves. They identified more clearly with teacher interests and began putting distance between themselves and administrators. Early in the 1970s, in an attempt to compete with the AFT's push for collective bargaining, the NEA urged all state legislatures to mandate "professional negotiations." Essentially a weaker form of bargaining, the NEA plan was rejected everywhere. In 1965 a somewhat similar plan had been attempted in California. Known as the Winton Act, the measure permitted teacher representatives to "meet and confer" on virtually all issues, but did not alter the school board's authority to make final decisions on those issues. Administrators were obligated to talk with teachers, but they were not obligated to take such advice as was offered.

The Winton Act did little to satisfy the desires of teachers for meaningful participation in the running of school systems. Neither did it provide for recognition of a single teacher organization, except in those locations where only one existed. In 1975 these objections were overcome by passage of Senate Bill 160, authored by Senator Albert S. Rodda. Before his election to the state senate in 1958, Rodda had been president of the California Federation of Teachers Local No. 31 in Sacramento. His measure had won the strong support of the Democratic governor and a legislature sympathetic to organized labor. Key provisions of the new law called for an Educational Employment Relations Board to implement the act, recognition and certification of a single employee organization as the exclusive representative of employees, binding arbitration of disputes, and mandatory negotiation for certain issues.[10]

The Rodda Act marked a milestone, but it was not a panacea. Nothing in the act could solve the most pressing of educational problems: inadequate financing, inequitable educational opportunity, and dwindling local control of schools.

CHAPTER SEVEN

Cultivating Higher Learning

EARLY IN 1849 Samuel H. Wiley, a Protestant clergyman from Monterey, in a conversation with Thomas O. Larkin, the former United States consul to California, proposed that a public university be established in California. Neither he nor Larkin were in a position to do anything immediately, but in the months and years that followed, Wiley acted on his ideals, first in his capacity as chaplain of the state's first constitutional convention and later as a founder of the College of California. Provisions in the state's first constitution, which he may have inspired, authorized the use of funds from the sale and rental of state lands to support a university.

In spite of constitutional authorization and the hope of some delegates that the legislature would act immediately to establish a university, the legislators gave first priority to the financing of elementary education. They did establish in their first session of 1851 a university board and mandated that a site valued at no less than $20,000 be acquired. The state supreme court was instructed to determine whether or not land offered to the university met the value test. The new trustees early acquired an offer of land in San Jose, but the supreme court found the offer unacceptable, a decision that took the momentum out of the drive for early action.

Public action having been frustrated, private initiative now came to the fore. Shortly after the conclusion of California's first legislative session, Samuel Wiley transferred his pastoral activities from Monterey to San Francisco where he established a close friendship with Henry Durant, a Yale graduate and a Congregational minister. By 1853, with the sponsorship of Wiley and four other Congregational and Presbyterian ministers, Durant began academy-level classes for three students at a house in Oakland. In 1855 the legislature approved a charter for Durant's academy, and the institution became known officially as the College of California. Until 1860, however, the college retained its identity as "Contra Costa Academy."[1]

For some years Durant, Wiley, and their small band of supporters had more space than students at the facility in Oakland, but they aspired nevertheless to acquire an ample and beautiful site. The new location, it was hoped, would be compatible with their vision of an institution possessing moral and intellectual greatness. In 1858 their aspirations were realized when they purchased a magnificent 140-acre site on both banks of Strawberry Creek in the Berkeley hills overlooking San Francisco Bay. Two years later the academy-level offerings of "Contra Costa Academy" finally gave way to college-level courses under the College of California, with Durant becoming the institution's first professor. The second professor was Martin Kellogg, pastor of the First Congregational Church at Grass Valley. Both men later became presidents of the University of California.

The eventual transformation of the private College of California into a state-supported institution was aided significantly by the federal Morrill Act of 1862. By its provisions each state received 30,000 acres of public land for each of its congressmen, the proceeds from the sale of the lands to be devoted to the establishment of colleges of agriculture and mechanical arts. In 1868 the California legislature created a commission for the "establishment of an agricultural, mining and mechanical arts college." Both San Jose and Napa were considered briefly as sites for the proposed state university, but it was President Henry Durant of the College of California who offered the most attractive proposition. He convinced the commission to merge the university with his institution and locate the new entity on the recently acquired site at Berkeley.

In response to Durant's wishes members of the college board

voted to convey to the University of California all their debts and assets, including the Berkeley site, and then to disincorporate. In March 1868 the legislature accepted the proposition. University classes were first offered in Oakland to thirty-eight students in September 1869. Four years later the university moved to its newly completed buildings in Berkeley.

The regents desired to broaden the mission, identity, and visibility of their new trust, and they sought as the university's first president a man of national stature. They settled first on General George B. McClellan, the well-known former commander of the Union Army during the Civil War. As McClellan was unpopular with the sizable number of southerners in California as well as with Republicans for having challenged Abraham Lincoln for the presidency in 1864, his decision to decline the appointment was probably in the best interest of all concerned. In 1870 the regents approached Daniel Coit Gilman, a reputable scholar at Yale's Sheffield Scientific School, but he too refused, citing heavy responsibilities in his present assignment. The regents then chose sixty-eight-year-old Henry Durant as the university's first president. The honor was acknowledgment of contributions already made, a fact he himself recognized when he resigned only two years later in favor of Daniel Coit Gilman, the same person who had earlier declined the job.

The difficulty in finding a president did not hamper the university's growth. In the 1870s the curriculum was expanded to include science and engineering. The university also received major private gifts, including the Toland Medical College in San Francisco and a professorship in Oriental languages. James Lick established a $700,000 trust fund toward the building and endowment of an observatory which was completed in 1888. Nine years earlier, in 1879, the Hastings College of Law had affiliated with the university. During these years the Berkeley campus took its modern architectural shape through an ambitious program of planning and building, spurred on in large measure by the substantial philanthropy of Phoebe Apperson Hearst.

The gifts and endowments encouraged recruitment of a creative faculty who won national and world recognition for their research and publications. At a special celebration in 1899 to honor the school's progress, Professor Joseph LeConte observed that "the University has become now an institution in which the professor is no longer a teacher merely, but also a maker of science and philosophy; and the relation is no longer one of teacher and learner, but also of co-worker in the field of thought."[2]

The progress did not come without turmoil which threatened relations between the presidents and the Board of Regents and among various academic and practical interests competing for prominence within the institution. Dissension arose over the relative virtues of literary, agricultural, and scientific departments, as well as over the use of funds for their support. Upon being offered the presidency in 1899, Benjamin Ide Wheeler, then professor of comparative philology at Cornell University, agreed to accept only on condition that the regents permit him to serve as the sole link of communication between faculty and regents, that he have the initiative in appointments and removal of faculty, and that the regents agree to support him in the discharge of his administrative duties. By restraining the influence of the regents in the everyday affairs of the university, Wheeler did much to end the factionalism that had beset the institution during its early years.[3] By seeking the best faculty, supporting department chairs, and fighting for good faculty salaries, he, more than any other president, set the university on the road to greatness.

Wheeler's strength also provided the seeds for his undoing during the faculty revolt of 1919–1920. The distinguished faculty he had brought to transform the university into a first-rate institution refused to be dominated by a president— even a great president. In the years that followed his retirement, the faculty, through its academic senate, gained nearly exclusive responsibility for courses and curricula and strong influence in personnel matters. But the direction of the university remained primarily in the hands of Wheeler's successors, aided by the regents, chancellors, and other administrative officers. By the 1930s, after three decades of recruiting faculty and developing libraries and laboratories, the University of California had entered the front rank of American universities. Central to its mission was a multifaceted program of undergraduate and graduate instruction, basic research, and service to the economic and cultural interests of the state.

Robert Gordon Sproul, President of the University of California, 1930–
1958. (*Photograph [circa* 1955] *courtesy of the Bancroft Library, University of
California, Berkeley.*)

While Wheeler set the university on its course to greatness,
his successors, particularly Robert Gordon Sproul, guided its
transition into a multicampus system. Sproul's long service included sixteen years in various administrative posts before serving twenty-eight years (1930–1958) as president. Some steps
toward expansion had already occurred under previous administrations, including the establishment of several research stations
outside Berkeley, a farm and school of agriculture at Davis, and,
in 1919, a major branch at Los Angeles, but Sproul presided
over an era of unprecedented growth.

Prior to assuming the presidency, Sproul had been instrumental in the development of UCLA, including the acquisition of its permanent site in Westwood. By the time he left office in 1958, the UCLA campus had become a major institution in its own right, enrolling nearly as many students as Berkeley. In addition, the program at Davis had been expanded significantly and new campuses had been developed at Santa Barbara and Riverside. More than any other leader in the university's history, Sproul had been able to convince the legislature—largely rural and Republican dominated during his presidency—that appropriations for the university paid handsome dividends for the state.

In a practical, service-oriented sense, the university's impact was felt on a broad diversity of fronts ranging from nuclear fission to nuclear medicine. Services were extended to the U.S. Department of Defense and giant corporations as well as to individual patients at teaching hospitals. The development of California agriculture followed in a significant way on the practical discoveries made by scholars on the Berkeley, Davis, Los Angeles, and Riverside campuses.

The university's dramatic growth during its first century was without precedent in the history of higher education: it had become a "multiversity," a term coined by university president Clark Kerr in 1963.[4] That growth continued during the 1960s with the addition of new campuses at Irvine, San Diego, and Santa Cruz. By 1970 the university had a full-time enrollment in excess of 100,000 students. More impressive than the size was the quality of the institution. In 1966 the American Council of Education characterized the Berkeley campus as the "best balanced, distinguished university in the country." Similar surveys in the later 1960s and in the 1970s have reaffirmed the earlier opinions of Berkeley's luster and proclaimed the emergence of UCLA among the nation's most distinguished universities. Besides its outstanding faculty, UCLA possesses the Jules Stein Eye Institute and the Brain Research Institute, both considered the best facilities of their kind in the world.

While the University of California was becoming a prominent force in the educational life of the state, other colleges and universities had also assumed responsibility for teaching thousands of students. Even prior to the efforts of Congregationalists and Presbyterians in founding the College of California, Methodists founded the College (later University) of the Pacific in 1851, permitting it to lay claim to being the longest-surviving collegiate-level institution in California. Within the first two decades of statehood, Catholics established five colleges in northern California (Santa Clara, San Francisco, St. Mary's, Notre Dame, College of Holy Names) and one in southern California (St. Vincent, later Loyola Marymount). Most private colleges possessing Catholic or Protestant roots sought to advance sectarian interests as well as the cause of general enlightenment.

Many colleges, including Mills (1885), Pomona (1887), Occidental (1887), Whittier (1901), and the University of Redlands (1906), to name but a few, focused on the development of a liberal arts curriculum for undergraduates. Their principal mission differed but slightly from the numerous colleges and universities maintained by Catholic and Protestant church groups, the only notable exception being the absence of a sectarian influence on the curriculum. Unlike the College of California, whose trustees voted to disincorporate in favor of the University of California, these institutions reflect the vitality of private educational efforts. Consistent with the American tradition of philanthropy, all private institutions owed their existence to the generosity of benefactors.

A relatively few private colleges and universities, particularly Stanford University (1885), the California Institute of Technology (founded as Throop Polytechnic Institute in 1891), and the University of Southern California (1880), have stressed research and the generation of new knowledge along with teaching. The oldest university in this group is USC which entered the ranks of major research universities comparatively recently, a transition generally associated with the appointment of Norman Topping as president in 1958. In earlier years USC's research orientation had rested primarily with its professional schools of law, medicine, and dentistry.[5] Between 1958 and 1979 the university expended more than $300 million on new facilities and expanded the number of its research faculty by several hundred. Private donors have given the university facilities at Idyllwild and Catalina Island, and a hospital-medical school that rivals the nation's largest.

The California Institute of Technology has emphasized scientific research since acquiring its present name in 1920. As one of the most distinguished scientific institutions in the nation, Caltech by 1978 could boast of 45 faculty members in the National Academy of Sciences and 24 in the National Academy of Engineering.[6] Special facilities, including the Palomar Observatory with its 200-inch telescope and the world-famous and independently operated Jet Propulsion Laboratory in Pasadena, are available to collect and analyze data on space.

The most colorful personality to lead higher education in California was probably David Starr Jordan, first president of Leland Stanford, Jr., University. Jordan served Stanford as president from its beginning in 1891 until his retirement in 1913, and as chancellor and chancellor emeritus from 1913 until his death in 1931. More involved in state and community affairs than most university presidents, Jordan acted as a major interpreter of higher education to the nation. Speaking out in behalf of American Indians, the coeducation of men and women, and in opposition to the segregation of Japanese students during the San Francisco school controversy, his was one of the education community's most notable voices for moral leadership. Through public lectures and books, he also articulated more clearly than most people what universities should be doing. "Original research is the loftiest function of the university," Jordan observed. "Those who do original work will train others to do it. Where the teachers are themselves original investigators devoted to truth and skillful in the search for it— men that cannot be frightened, fatigued, or discouraged—they will have students like themselves."[7] As a rule, he held to the traditional view that higher education required students to leave home and become part of a "guild of scholars."

From the beginning Jordan spoke of creating an institution "of the highest grade." If the expression of such grand aspirations is almost commonplace in the founding of universities, realizing them is not. Over the past ninety years Stanford University has become one of the nation's most distinguished institutions for higher learning and research. With an enrollment by the late 1970s of slightly more than 13,000 students, that distinction did not come from size, but from the achievements of its faculty. In a recent survey conducted by Everett C. Ladd, Jr., and Seymour Lipset, Stanford was acknowledged to be one of America's five best universities in seventeen fields, a distinction it shared only with the University of California, Berkeley.[8] Its school of education has been acclaimed as the nation's most distinguished in every major survey conducted during the past decade.

Research at Stanford in particle physics, cancer therapy, and heart disease has been on the cutting edge of scientific achievement. Since 1966 the campus's two-mile linear accelerator has made possible pioneering studies in the electromagnetic structure of the proton. Impressive studies in the interrelationships between computer science and communications technologies have been undertaken at the Stanford Research Institute.

Advanced scholarship in the humanities and the social sciences at Stanford, Berkeley, UCLA, and other universities has been made possible by the development in California of numerous research libraries, archives, and museums. Most have been developed by the universities themselves, frequently with aid from private benefactors. The largest of the research libraries is found on the University of California's campus at Berkeley. Notable among the nearly two dozen libraries at Berkeley is the Bancroft, which houses manuscript and rare book collections on the history of western North America, Mexico, and colonial Latin America, and on California authors. Distinguished as well are holdings nearly as massive at UCLA and Stanford, including Stanford's Hoover Institution on War, Revolution, and Peace. and UCLA's William Andrews Clark Memorial Library, featuring rare books on seventeenth- and eighteenth-century English civilization. Particularly noteworthy among the private libraries is the Henry E. Huntington Library and Art Gallery in Pasadena. Featured there are manuscripts and rare books pertaining to English history and literature, colonial American history, and early California.

Research-oriented universities, with their distinguished faculties, laboratories, and libraries, contributed much to the material and cultural development of California and Californians, but they were not inclined to assume primary responsibility for preparing teachers to serve the great majority of California children. During the nineteenth century the teacher preparation function had been assumed by special-purpose "normal schools" of a subcollegiate level. John Swett, among others, had repeatedly reminded school boards that their instructional programs could be only as good as the teachers they hired. In 1862 California became the ninth state to establish a normal school for the training of teachers. Opened originally in San Francisco in July 1862, the school emphasized both subject-matter knowledge and teaching techniques.

The need for trained teachers assured the growth and expansion of normal schools. In 1871 the normal school moved from San Francisco to its permanent site in San Jose. A decade later a branch opened in Los Angeles, and in 1887 another in Chico. Subsequent normal schools were not considered branches of the one at San Jose, but enjoyed separate identities. These schools included campuses at San Diego (1897), San Francisco (1899), Santa Barbara (1909), Fresno (1911), and Arcata (Humboldt State) in 1913. As the mission of higher education expanded during the first half of the twentieth century, the normal schools at Los Angeles and Santa Barbara were brought into the University of California system for demographic and political reasons. The remainder became teachers' colleges (1921), then state colleges (1935), and ultimately campuses of the California State University and Colleges system (1962).[9] This system now includes nineteen separate campuses with a student enrollment exceeding a quarter of a million.

The evolution of the state university and colleges from normal schools to comprehensive university centers followed a pattern similar to that established by state teacher preparatory institutions in most other states. By 1899 the normal schools had come under the jurisdiction of the State Board of Education, but for two decades thereafter they also retained local governing boards. By abolishing the local boards in 1920, the legislature moved toward establishment of a statewide system of teachers' colleges, an action formally taken in 1921. With a changed administrative structure came a modification in mission. The colleges expanded their curricula to include a greater emphasis on general education, the liberal arts, and sciences. A formal recognition of this transformation occurred in 1935 when the legislature renamed the teacher preparation institutions "state colleges," specifically approved the establishment of curricula other than teacher education, and eliminated for graduation all course requirements in education. Lest anyone assume that the broadening trend was becoming uncontrollable, the legislature re-

PUBLIC FOUR YEAR AND GRADUATE INSTITUTIONS OF
HIGHER EDUCATION IN CALIFORNIA.

Public four-year and graduate institutions of higher education in California.

affirmed that the primary function of the state colleges was the training of teachers for the elementary schools.

Shortly after the turn of the century the junior college was added to the galaxy of higher education institutions in California. While the junior college was not conceived in California, it reached there its most complete development. During the last half of the nineteenth century several presidents of major mid-western universities had argued that some early university courses should be moved into the high schools. In 1892 William Rainey Harper, president of the University of Chicago, divided the four-year undergraduate program into two divisions. In 1896 the first, or lower of these divisions (comprising the freshman and sophomore years), because known as the "junior college." This was the first known use of the term. Harper encouraged high schools to offer one or two years of lower-division collegiate-level study as a capstone to their regular offerings. With Harper's encouragement the first public junior college was established under local authority at Joliet, Illinois, in 1902.

Five years later, in 1907, California became the first state to enact legislation establishing junior colleges. Authored by Senator Anthony Caminetti of Amador Country, the act authorized—but did not require—local trustees of high school districts to provide post–high school courses approximating the level of courses found in the first two years of college. In 1910 Fresno High School became the first to offer such courses, followed by Santa Barbara High School in 1911. In 1913 Fullerton Junior College was organized when two years of post-graduate work were added to the offerings of Fullerton High School. Within a year similar two-year colleges were organized in Los Angeles, Santa Monica, Long Beach, Santa Barbara, Auburn, and Bakersfield.[10]

California's implementation of the junior college movement was attributable in large measure to the work of Alex F. Lange, director of the School of Education at the University of California. As chairman of the university's Commission on Readjustment of Courses of Study, Lange and his committee reached the same conclusion drawn by President Harper at Chicago nearly twenty years earlier. This encouragement from the University of California helped make the junior college the capstone to the state's public school system.

Until 1960 junior colleges were regarded as part of the secondary school program of the state and were organized and supported like high schools and elementary schools. In 1921 the legislature had approved state funding for junior colleges and mandated open admissions. By doing so the junior colleges not only reduced the enrollment pressure on the University of California and the teachers' colleges but dramatically increased access to higher education for Californians. The extraordinary expansion of these institutions after World War II left virtually every community with its own junior college.

From the beginning, most junior colleges offered both academic and vocational courses. The rise of vocational studies corresponded closely with passage of the Smith-Hughes Act of 1917. Federal funding supplied by that legislation not only produced a broadening of the high school and junior college curricula, it also stimulated administrative changes, including night classes and part-time schedules. Under the Master Plan of 1960, vocational and technical education became the exclusive province of the junior colleges, neither of the other two systems of higher education being assigned that function.

Given diversity in number, type, and funding source of California's collegiate-level institutions, the emergence of rivalry in the higher education community was not surprising. The influx of population after World War II produced a near doubling of collegiate enrollment. By 1960 more than sixty percent of the youth recently graduated from high school were continuing their education with some sort of formal postsecondary schooling. While there appeared to be an ample number of students for all public institutions, competition for students, programs, dollars, and even campuses produced what Arthur G. Coons, former president of Occidental College, described as a frequently "depressing and outright disgusting" political process.[11] Often the location of a college or university campus in a community was inspired by real estate developers and businesses. Their aspirations were not always consistent with present and future needs, as evidenced in 1955 by a state senate bill which sought unsuccessfully to establish eight new state colleges, all north of the Tehachapi mountains where population growth was slowest.

By 1959 it had become apparent that the growth of higher education had to be managed intelligently. Concern over duplication of facilities and cost had been expressed earlier. In 1933 the Suzzalo Report of the Carnegie Foundation for the Advancement of Teaching had recommended that all public higher education in California be placed under the authority of the University of California regents. Two subsequent studies, the Strayer Report of 1938 and the McConnell Report of 1955, also emphasized the need for coordination and planning.

During the 1959 legislative session, twenty-three bills, three resolutions, and two constitutional amendments were introduced relating to higher education, many advancing extreme proposals. In the end it was Assembly Concurrent Resolution 88, authored by Dorothy M. Donahoe of Bakersfield, that received approval. Her resolution called for creation of a liaison committee, consisting of University of California regents and representatives of the State Board of Education, to "prepare a master plan for the development, expansion, and integration of the facilities, curriculum, and standards of higher education" in California.

Under the capable leadership of Arthur G. Coons, the committee completed its work late in 1959. Its Master Plan was approved as Senate Bill 33 at a special session of the 1960 legislature and has guided higher education policy in California ever since. Endorsed by all major higher education entities in the state, it has served as a model for the rational planning of higher education committees elsewhere in the nation. Most significant among the Master Plan's achievements was a definition of eligibility for admission to the state's public institutions, and a differentiation of institutional missions. Specifically, on the issue of student admission, this plan stipulated that "the state colleges select first-time freshmen from the top one-third (33⅓ percent) and the University from the top one-eighth (12½ percent) of all graduates of California public high schools."[12] By becoming more selective in their admissions standards, the university and state colleges deflected substantial responsibility for lower division enrollment to the junior colleges. This planning assured all graduates from accredited high schools admission to college somewhere within California's public higher educational system.

As for the differentiated missions, the University of California was entrusted with responsibility for research. It was given "exclusive" jurisdiction over instruction in law and graduate instruction in medicine, dentistry, veterinary medicine, and architecture as well as "sole authority" to award the doctoral degree in all fields, "except that it may agree with the state colleges to award joint doctoral degrees in selected fields." The "primary function" of state colleges was to provide undergraduate and graduate education in all fields and at all levels not left exclusively to the university. The junior colleges were required to offer liberal arts instruction not beyond the fourteenth grade as well as vocational and technical programs leading to employment.

Results being achieved under the Master Plan ten years following its implementation were in large measure consistent with the original design. The ninety-five public "community colleges," to use the term that succeeded "junior colleges" in the nomenclature of higher education, served over 600,000 students and assumed principal responsibility for the first two collegiate years. Similarly, the nineteen campuses of the California State University and Colleges system have assumed a steadily increasing share of the undergraduate enrollment. By the late 1970s well over half of the bachelor's degrees and over a third of the master's degrees awarded annually in California were granted by the CSUC campuses. Eight campuses in that system enrolled over 20,000 students each. Three campuses, those at San Diego, Long Beach, and San Jose, each with annual enrollments exceeding 30,000, were comparable in size to the University of California campuses at Berkeley and Los Angeles.

As the nation's most populated state, with the largest enrollment of postsecondary students, California's expenditure for higher education vies only with New York state as the highest in the nation. Yet in 1968–1969 California ranked in the lower half of the nation in the proportion of personal income spent on higher education; only 2.08 percent of that income went to higher education.[13] Since California ranks first in the nation in the ratio of students remaining in the state after taking credits toward bachelor's degrees, its citizens are gaining a favorable return on their higher-education dollars.

Beyond mandating functions for the three public systems, the Master Plan recognized officially the role of private colleges and universities in the educational process through the establishment of a Coordinating Council for Higher Education. Such recognition was sorely needed since increasing costs and competition from public institutions had been threatening the existence of many private colleges. By 1970 the private sector accounted for only a little over ten percent of the 1,255,732 students enrolled in California's institutions of higher learning.[14]

The Coordinating Council, including representatives from

both public and private higher education, was charged with recommending new campuses and programs for the public sector. In 1974 it gave way to a new planning group, the California Postsecondary Education Commission. While the Commission, like the Coordinating Council before it, operates only in an advisory capacity to the legislature, it has authority to demand information from the various public segments of higher education, a power not enjoyed by its predecessor. It also has authority to pass upon all proposals for new college and university campuses before those suggestions are considered by the legislature.

The Master Plan appears to have achieved its main purposes: each of the three systems fulfills a special function, with appropriate opportunities being made available to all students seeking higher education. But not even the Master Plan could have anticipated the social and political difficulties inherent in admissions policy. As educators and the public became sensitive to the underrepresentation of minority students on college and university campusees, they instituted various special admissions programs and opportunities for financial assistance. Minority representation did improve, even in the most selective of the state systems, though not as much as many had wished. In 1968 Mexican Americans represented 1.6 percent of the University of California's student enrollment. By 1972 their percentage had increased to 4.8. Similarly, between 1968 and 1972, the percentage of blacks rose from 2.1 to 5.2, that of Asian Americans from 5.2 to 8.3. Only in the case of American Indians was the improvement negligible, rising from 0.2 to 0.6 percent.[15] Minority enrollment continued to increase after 1972, but at a much slower rate. In the case of blacks, their percentage actually declined. In the fall of 1978 the university's undergraduates included 3.8 percent blacks, 11.4 percent Asians and Pacific Islanders, 5.5 percent Hispanics, and 0.4 percent American Indians.[16]

Advances in minority admissions did not come easily. In the 1970s California occupied center attention in the nation's most celebrated court test of special admissions programs. Partially affirming a California supreme court ruling in *Regents of the University of California* v. *Allan Bakke,* the U.S. Supreme Court decided in June 1978 that the special admissions program at the

Davis Medical School was not constitutionally adequate.[17] Although taking care to uphold the constitutionality of special admissions programs, the judges thought that Allan Bakke had been wrongfully denied admission because the university had reserved a fixed number of places in its entering class for minority students. Race could be considered as one factor in the admissions process, the court ruled, but a specific quota of spaces could not be reserved for a particular group of students.

While its decision sent mixed signals into the community of higher education, the court steered a cautious course. A strongly worded decision against what some journalists and Bakke supporters referred to as "reverse discrimination" almost certainly would have placed all special admissions programs in jeopardy, thereby making it more difficult for higher education to open its doors to minorities and the poor.

Social Justice and Financing the Schools: The 1960s and 1970s

S YMBOLIC OF AN ANGRY and change-prone era in the history of California was the unrest that gripped many university campuses during the 1960s. These disturbances were partly aimed at university policies, particularly the increased remoteness of faculty from students, but most discontent was caused by societal problems, particularly the highly unpopular war in Vietnam, the continued use of the military draft, American businesses producing the instruments of war, and various causes that related to minority housing and employment. Regardless of the reasons for the protests, the public watched student demonstrations with complete disdain, and were ready to penalize the University of California when students disrupted classes and destroyed public property. A by-product of the turbulence was greater student influence on educational policy gained through their membership— though generally without vote— on various university committees.

Student rebelliousness on college campuses had only a limited influence on educational policy in the public elementary and secondary schools. For the public schools the major concern was growth, which was far more basic to the problems of large cities and their surrounding suburbs. By 1976–1977 approximately two-thirds of California's public-school students were registered in only 258 unified school districts, with 784 elementary and high school districts accommodating the remaining third. Five large districts—Los Angeles, Long Beach, Oakland, San Diego, and San Francisco—enrolled twenty percent of all public school students in the state. Los Angeles alone, with over 600,000 pupils, had nearly fourteen percent of the total. Less than nine percent of the elementary and secondary level enrollment was in private schools.[1]

Although school enrollment grew dramatically between 1940 and 1977, the number of school systems declined from 2,817 to 1,042.[2] In 1935 there had been 3,865 public schools serving approximately 660,000 students. By 1967 the number of schools had nearly doubled to 6,817 while enrollment had increased more than eightfold to about 5,465,000.[3] Greater enrollments and urbanization produced dramatic changes in school organization, but did not completely eliminate the one-room schoolhouse, a legacy of an earlier day. As late as 1977 California's rural communities were still maintaining 55 one-room schools.

The change from smaller to larger schools did not result entirely from urbanization. A need to improve efficiency, control school costs, and equalize services from one community to another seemed to require larger schools and districts. As late as 1935 there had been no unified schools districts in California, i.e., districts responsible for all public school of grades kindergarten through twelve. During World War II Governor Earl Warren established a Commission for Post-War Planning, which recommended the consolidation of elementary and high school districts. Such consolidations were to create unified districts responsible for schooling all children from kindergarten through twelfth grade. The movement toward unification grew slowly after the war, receiving acceptance primarily in large cities. Legislation mandating consolidation in 1964 boosted the number of unified districts from 119 in 1960 to 240 in 1970.

As enrollment increased in urban schools, the public became increasingly estranged from school leaders. Early in 1960 an article appeared in a national education magazine reporting a "conservative revolution" in California education.[4] While schools were continuing to win the public's financial support, criticism of alleged "fads and frills" in the curriculum was becoming more common. In 1962, with the election of the conservative Max Rafferty as state superintendent of public instruction, Californians appeared to be endorsing their candidate's basic education message as captured in his billboard slogan: "Reading, Riting, Rafferty."

Sixteen years later there was ample evidence that the public still held basic education in favor, though without Rafferty, the latter having been turned aside by the voters in 1970 when he sought reelection as state superintendent. Disaffection with Rafferty did not imply disaffection with his basic education message. Lack of discipline, use of drugs by students, poor financial support, integration/busing, and poor curriculum standards constituted the five leading problems identified by the public as facing the schools nationally. While a majority of respondents still believed that the public schools were doing a good job, that percentage had declined from what it had been a decade earlier. A national survey conducted in 1978 revealed that westerners— those living in the area embracing the Rocky Mountain and Pacific Coast states— were least satisfied with the public schools. But like citizens elsewhere, those who had children in public schools were far more supportive of the schools than those who did not.[5]

Public uneasiness about the state's school system prompted the legislature to intervene frequently, but not always wisely, in education matters. During the early 1960s most of the legislative effort went toward strengthening the academic side of the public school curriculum and the preparation of teachers. Through Assembly Bill 2565, approved in 1961, the legislature not only specified subjects of instruction, but also reorganized the curriculum. English was separated from the social studies, the latter to be taught as geography and history rather than as a unity of numerous subjects. English classes had to include grammar and literature, while instruction was required in civics, a foreign language or languages, natural sciences, and health— all of this to begin not later than grade six and continue through the end of elementary schooling. Because few elementary teachers were competent in foreign languages, school officials were faced with implementing a nearly impossible requirement.

As the public during the 1960s became more assured about the nation's capability in science and technology, political pressure on the curriculum shifted to practical subjects. California schools, like schools throughout the nation, benefited markedly from congressional passage of the Elementary and Secondary Education Act of 1965. That legislation, expressed in three major programs, was aimed at (1) providing assistance for the education of children from low-income families; (2) providing library resources, textbooks, and instructional materials to schools in low-wealth areas; and (3) establishing supplementary educational centers and services in areas with a concentration of low-income families. Local school systems initiated literally hundreds of projects designed to stimulate programs in reading, bilingual education, English language, multicultural education, the social studies, and many other subjects. Stimulation from the federal government also led to increased state interest in the curriculum, especially in reading and bilingual education, as well as programs for the children of migrant farm workers.

But the state was more interested in making the schools establish standards of education than in developing new programs. In 1969 the legislature approved "minimum academic standards for graduation" and in 1977 approved strict competency standards for high school graduation. As a result of A.B. 3408, sponsored by Assemblyman Gary K. Hart of Santa Barbara, students receiving a high school diploma after June 1980 had to demonstrate minimal proficiency, as determined by a local board, in reading, writing, and computational skills.

These changes in education were extensive, but not all of them were the result of government-mandated programs. Indeed, the accountability movement may have received more support in university halls than in the legislature. Clearly the movement could not have gone as far as it did without the work of educational theorists who urged teachers to specify and measure the skills and knowledge they expected students to acquire. Other newer trends in education, such as team teaching and various approaches to individualizing instruction, were the products of creative thought by university scholars in education. Such reforms were generally well received by the public which welcomed more effective approaches in instruction, especially in the basic subjects.

But educational reforms did not rank as high in the public mind as the desire for lower school taxes. In terms of direct citizen action, school financing has attracted the most attention. Before 1978 communities differed greatly in the amount of local property tax they collected for the support of schools. Even when the state's contribution to school financing was considered, the per pupil expenditures still varied enormously from one community to another. In 1967, for example, the per pupil expenditure for elementary and secondary students in the public schools of Los Angeles averaged $601 as compared to $1,192 in Beverly Hills, $984 in Palo Alto, and $693 in San Francisco.[6]

Differences between tax rates and assessed valuation from community to community assured that inequality would prevail in the support of public schooling. Over the years steps were taken to effect partial remedies. The governor's Commission for Postwar Planning had recommended legislation to equalize school financing. The state's response was a constitutional amendment and the Fair Equalization Law of 1945, which alleviated some, but not all of the unfairness by providing school districts with three types of state aid. Between 1945 and 1972, "basic aid" was allotted in the form of a set amount per pupil in average daily attendance ($125 for much of the period). In addition, those districts wherein assessed valuation fell below a certain prescribed amount received "equalization aid." Finally, especially poor districts obtained "supplemental aid" according to a similar formula.[7] The total state contribution amounted to about half the expenditure for school support.

While the state based a substantial portion of its contribution on the needs of a particular school district, enormous inequities still remained as a result of the differing amounts of local taxes collected for schools. The essential unfairness of the system led in 1971 to the California supreme court decision in *Serrano* v. *Priest.*[8] John Serrano, a resident of Baldwin Park and plaintiff in the case, believed that his son was being treated unfairly. Given the facts as presented in 1968, specifically that the Baldwin Park Unified School District was spending only $577 per year on each pupil while some other Los Angeles County districts were spending more than twice that amount, the court had little difficulty finding in favor of Serrano. The court held that parents, pupils, and taxpayers in low-wealth districts were being denied equal protection of the law because California's system of allocating financial support to school districts permitted great inequalities to exist. Even though state aid had been distributed more equitably than ever before, the state still permitted the amount of local revenue raised from property tax to determine the budgets of school districts.

As early as 1972, through passage of Senate Bill 90, the legislature began to cope, however modestly, with the spirit of *Serrano* v. *Priest*. The major feature of that legislation had been the imposition annually of revenue limits on school districts, thereby controlling the amount of general-purpose tax produced for local school support. Five years later, in approving a comprehensive school finance bill, the legislature moved closer to full compliance with the court mandate. The court had not required all school districts to spend the same amount on each child, nor had it decreed that local property taxes could not be used as a means of financing public schools, but in its final review of the case in December 1976, known as Serrano II, the court held that differences in the annual expenditure per pupil could not exceed $100.[9]

At the same time as equality in the financing of schools was receiving attention, a revolt arose against high property taxes in the state. Despite modest legislative efforts after World War II to reform the financing of public education, more than half of California's school funds came from local property taxes. Dissatisfaction with those taxes, including the old objection of paying taxes, especially high taxes, to educate other people's children, led to frequent defeats of local efforts to increase property tax rates for operating schools. Between 1966 and 1970, nearly half of the local tax-increase elections in California were lost, as were sixty percent of the school bond elections. The public emphasized its displeasure by defeating the same proposals time and again, and often by large majorities.

By 1978 the resentment against high property taxes had become acute. The rapid appreciation of values in California, especially in Los Angeles County, had resulted in dramatic increases in property tax bills for homeowners. Led by a veteran southern California tax fighter, Howard A. Jarvis, the electorate in June 1978 overwhelmingly approved Proposition 13, an amendment to the state's constitution limiting the tax on property to one percent of fair market value. Years of debate over the implications of *Serrano* v. *Priest* notwithstanding, the voters of California had summarily produced a radical shift in the financing of public education.

Although a conservative reaction against property taxes rather than an attempt at educational reform, Proposition 13 did have major implications for school policy. By severely limiting local property tax revenue for school support, the amendment provided additional incentive for the state to assume a greater portion of school costs, and presumably to do so on a basis of equality as mandated in *Serrano.* During the 1978–1979 school year, over 65 percent of the school revenue came from the state, as contrasted with less than 45 percent during 1977–1978.

Another impact of Proposition 13 may well be an accelerated weakening of local authority over schools. Since the turn of the century, the state, particularly the legislature, has been gaining influence over education at the expense of local communities. Detailed administrative controls and policy directives applicable to the state board of education, county boards of education, and local school districts are embodied in the *Education Code,* consisting in 1976 of some 80,000 sections compiled into eight volumes. Much of the legislation concerns the organization, support, and governance of education, but the legislature has proven quite willing to intervene in curricular matters as well. Literally hundreds of sections in the *Code* define courses of study that are required, authorized but not required, or prohibited. Generally speaking, legislatively mandated curriculum has resulted in great pressure on the limited time and resources available to a school district.

On occasion the legislature has removed some requirements that have proven unworkable. Such, for example, was the case with a requirement instituted during the early 1960s that foreign languages be taught in the elementary schools. Few elementary teachers were competent in foreign languages. Moreover, the legislature was not sufficiently motivated to appropriate funds for the massive in-service education effort that would have been needed to prepare teachers for carrying out the mandate. A decade later the requirement gave way to a mildly worded stricture that districts offer foreign languages "as early as feasible."[10]

State concerns over the curriculum, and even financing the schools, were overshadowed during much of the sixties and seventies by the issue of racial segregation. The state had legislated frequently on minority groups, especially Asians, but black citizens in particular had begun raising questions about segregation which proved especially troubling. The urbanization of an essentially rural black population occurred later in California than in the eastern part of the nation. In California's population of 3,426,861 in 1920, only 38,763 were black.[11] Even so, the number represented a 79.1 percent increase between 1910 and 1920.

During the succeeding decade, blacks still did not rush to California in large numbers, although their percentage increase in Los Angeles was comparable to that found in the great cities of the Northeast. While Los Angeles's 38,894 black residents in 1930 were few enough to avoid the intense crowding and concentration of poverty felt in the larger industrial cities of the East, they did constitute a presence that would not go unnoticed by whites. As blacks continued to move west during the depression decade of the 1930s, their number in Los Angeles rose to 63,774 by 1940.[12] By 1960 the total nonwhite population of Los Angeles was 417,000, but even with that substantial growth the number amounted to only 17 percent of the total. Among California's large cities, only Oakland had a minority population as large as 26 percent. In the decade to follow, these statistics would change dramatically.

Problems encountered in bringing nonwhites and Mexican Americans into the mainstream of California society involved institutions other than schools and involved strategies other than school desegregation. Owing in part to decisions of the courts, particularly the U.S. Supreme Court's decision in *Brown* v. *Board of Education* (1954), school desegregation offered a particularly hopeful opportunity for a major breakthrough. But few Californians believed the decision had much importance for solving educational problems in the state. That attitude persisted into the 1960s. Even after the devastating destruction brought by Los Angeles's Watts riots in August 1965, solutions proposed by the McCone Commission, an official "blue ribbon" body charged by Governor Edmund G. Brown with recommending corrective actions, did not include an attack on segregation. Rather, the commission recommended a costly compensatory educational program involving intensive instruction in small classes and more remedial courses, all conducted in the ghetto itself.

As the public became more conscious of the longstanding discrimination plaguing minority citizens, the desire for change increased. Minorities had been ignored in state-approved textbooks, denied access to job training programs, and, most important of all, refused opportunities to participate in the nation's economic system. Schools could play a role in helping to correct economic inequities, but that fundamental problem extended well beyond their capacity and jurisdiction. To be sure, some gains were being realized. Discrimination in government-sponsored job training programs was ending. The Federal Vocational Education Act of 1963, amended in 1976, made training benefits available to all, including non-English-speaking, economically disadvantaged, and physically handicapped persons. Unfortunately, unlike what had been the experience of whites for more than a century, improved educational opportunities for minorities were not always translated into improved job opportunities.

Certain problems involving race were related rather directly to the curriculum, particularly the underrepresentation of nonwhites in textbooks. Rarely did textbook authors engage in the outright untruthful portrayal of minorities as much as simply ignoring them and failing to report the many ways in which they had been discriminated against by the majority culture. In late 1963, the Berkeley chapter of the Congress of Racial Equality sponsored a study of the treatment accorded blacks in American history textbooks. The study, which was conducted by a group of prominent historians, all on the faculty of the University of California, Berkeley, concluded that blacks had been often neglected in history texts and recommended that the inequity be redressed. In March 1964, Kenneth M. Stampp, a noted historian of the Civil War and Reconstruction era, presented copies of the panel's report to the State Board of Education. The report so impressed the board that it acted immediately on the panel's recommendations. Copies of the document, *The Negro in American History Textbooks,* were sent to textbook publishers, the California Curriculum Commission, and the public schools.

By 1965 all American history textbooks submitted for state adoption in California were expected to give fair representation to minorities. The tangible impact of the new policy became vivid with the adoption of *Land of the Free,* an eighth-grade text authored by historians John W. Caughey of UCLA, John Hope Franklin of the University of Chicago, and Ernest R. May of Harvard University. Affirmative contributions of minorities were portrayed to an extent unprecedented in a major text, as were historical injustices toward minorities and foreign nations, features that drew heated attack from ultraconservative groups. During the following decade, human sensitivities would be sharpened by the state's curriculum guidelines, including a demand for greater recognition of female social roles and the contributions of women to history.

Even with improved recognition of minorities in textbooks, the challenge of bringing them into the mainstream of California life centered on policies designed to end school desegregation. That segregation was present, no one could deny. By 1970 more than 150,000 black children, 37 percent of the statewide total, were attending schools that were 90 percent or more black. According to the state's ethnic survey of school districts for 1970–1971, nearly 59 percent of the black pupils attended predominantly black schools, and nearly 29 percent of Spanish surname pupils attended predominantly Spanish surname schools.[13]

Necessarily, in order for desegregation to begin, a basic commitment for change had to be accepted by political and school leaders and the public that supported them. In 1962 the State Board of Education had encouraged desegregation, but almost no affirmative steps were taken until the mid-1960s. The first major break came in 1965 when the Riverside Unified School District, responding to the indignation of local blacks and the loss of a school through an arson-caused fire, adopted a plan that provided for racial balance in the district's twenty-five elementary schools. It was the nation's first full-scale plan implemented in a city with a population exceeding 100,000, and it was a tribute to local black citizens who had become disenchanted with weak attempts to deal with inequality through a voluntary transfer plan and a compensatory education program.

Although it was the first, the Riverside plan of busing only black and Mexican American children was less bold than Berkeley's plan which included white children as well. Beginning in 1964 Berkeley officials desegregated the city's three junior high schools. Four years later they added all elementary schools to the program, an impressive achievement in view of the fact that nearly 50 percent of the district was nonwhite as compared to Riverside where it was 18 percent.

There were other bright spots. Effective local leadership, state pressure, and encouragement from local nonwhites combined on occasion to produce positive results elsewhere. Several medium-size school districts in northern Orange County, like those in Fullerton, Placentia, and La Habra, moved to end segregation of Mexican American students. Other communities with relatively small predominantly nonwhite schools, such as Hanford, Merced, Monrovia, San Mateo, and Sausalito, also achieved desegregation. By closing inefficient and segregated facilities, these and other smaller communities integrated their schools with little or no difficulty.

In the larger cities, where the bulk of the state's minority enrollment resided, the difficulties were frequently extreme. Struggles for desegregation were intense and progress slow. Virtually all gains were incomplete and won only through lengthy litigation and complex political struggles. Such was the case in Pasadena, San Diego, San Francisco, and, most critically, in Los Angeles.

The legal issues differed in the major cities, but the basic decisions were grounded on *Brown* v. *Board of Education.* The several courts held that segregation, even if not deliberate, meant unequal educational opportunities. At issue in every case was the extent to which a local school board was obligated to correct the inequality. Necessarily, questions of feasibility, including cost and pupil welfare, weighed heavily in court decisions and plans to effect remedies. Given the deeply controversial nature of legally mandated school desegregation, the resolution of conflict rarely came easily.

What appeared to some citizens as a matter of simple justice—

permission for minority children to enjoy the same educational opportunities as those enjoyed by the children of the majority—became a deeply divisive social and emotional issue with ramifications well beyond the schools. Lost in the frenzied debate over desegregation was society's obligation to dispense school services equally among its citizens, the courts having determined repeatedly that this could not be done in racially isolated schools. In a sense, even the subject of the debate became distorted. Frequently persons did not claim to be divided on the issue of desegregation, but merely on the issue of "busing," the means frequently required to achieve desegregation. For many white parents, the immediate fear and resentment of having their children bused out of their own neighborhoods and into the less familiar inner city caused them to turn against the public schools.

Although the constitutional mandate for desegregation was clear, local school board members and administrators frequently were guided more by the difficulties of implementing a practical desegregation plan than by their legal obligation. The scenario, as characterized by the experiences in Los Angeles, was a commitment to desegregation as early as 1963, a denial of wrongdoing by the board, and then gradual implementation of one or more voluntary desegregation plans. Effective desegregation was constantly postponed, and even the decision in 1970 in *Crawford* v. *Los Angeles Board of Education,* which called for an end to *de facto* segregation (the segregation resulting from housing patterns rather than deliberate discrimination in the school system), did not produce immediate results.

Not until September 1978 did the Los Angeles school board attempt to implement the Crawford decision. Even then it began with a limited mandatory desegregation plan which sought to reassign about 85,000 students, almost a fifth of the total, to schools outside their neighborhoods. Unfortunately, the reassignments were not complied with by most white parents. An apparent practical constraint against lasting desegregation was the shifting nature of the population, the "browning of the cities," as it was sometimes called. When the Los Angeles desegregation issue emerged in 1963, an overwhelming majority of children in the district were white. By 1977 whites represented only 34 percent of the population, with their percentage

declining yearly. How much of that decline was directly attributable to "white flight," presumably for the purposes of avoid-
ing desegregation and/or busing, and how much was attributable
to birth rates and other demographic factors remains to be
studied by social scientists.

One recent manifestation of the busing controversy and other
dissatisfactions with public schools has been a marked increase
in private school enrollment. In the late 1970s, at a time when
public elementary (grades 1–8) and secondary (grades 9–12)
school enrollment was declining, private school enrollment at
those levels reached nearly twelve percent of the total school
enrollment in the state, increasing from 364,666 in 1973 to
425,850 in 1978.[14] Over 85 percent of the private school enrollment in 1973 and 77 percent in 1978 was in parochial
schools, operated primarily by the Catholic church.

With private schools assuming a larger share of the student
enrollment, parents of private-school pupils began to demonstrate increased interest in obtaining financial assistance from
the state. By 1979 major attention was focusing on the state's
"Initiative for Family Choice," a proposed constitutional amendment which proponents were seeking to qualify for the 1980
ballot. If approved by the electorate, the measure would provide state certificates to families which would be redeemable for
the full cost of education. Public schools were still favored in
that they would be targeted to receive about eleven percent
greater revenue than the voucher schools. At issue was the
traditional constitutional question of government aid to parochial schools, the historic issue of equality, and a full range of
less dramatic issues relating to state control of educational standards. Under terms of the initiative the state would be prohibited from extending controls over private schools beyond
those in effect on July 1, 1979, a level that, among other things,
did not include the licensure of teachers.[15]

Dissatisfaction with the public schools was expressed in other
ways as well. In 1970, long before the family choice initiative
was conceived, a rare coalition of blacks, who sought greater
control of their neighborhood schools, and conservative whites,
who wished to avoid desegregation, led to a legislative attempt
to reorganize the Los Angeles Unified School District into
smaller regional entities. Approved in the 1970 regular session

as Senate Bill 242, the move was thwarted only by Governor Ronald Reagan's veto. The governor was persuaded by Los Angeles school officials that the measure was unwise. Among other things, it mandated unnecessary interference by the state in the affairs of a local school district.

Desegregated schooling was the most controversial of several contemporary devices designed during the sixties and seventies to reduce the educational disadvantages of minority children from low-income homes, but it was not the only one. Passage in 1965 of the federal Elementary and Secondary Education Act and the state's Miller-Unruh Reading Act stimulated a host of efforts to help children improve their basic educational skills. By-products included reduction in the size of classes, special tutorial assistance, the assignment of reading specialists, and the augmentation of library resources. By the 1970s educators and legislators, spurred on by leaders from the Mexican American community, had responded to changes in the California population by placing a heavy emphasis on the design and funding of bilingual education programs. Parents also called on educators to become sensitive to the special needs of children with learning handicaps.

Notable among the state plans implemented during the past decade has been the Early Childhood Education Program initiated by State Superintendent of Public Instruction Wilson Riles and signed into law in November 1972. The program was based on the belief that a high proportion of a child's intelligence is developed prior to the age of eight and that even minor improvements in a school program can make an important difference in student achievement during the earlier years of schooling. In order to achieve improved educational results, a heavy emphasis was placed on assessing the child's needs and individualizing instruction to fit those needs, two ideas rooted deeply in the progressive education movement of a half century earlier.

Individualizing instruction to cope with the needs of normal students was not a new idea in education, but applying the concept to students with special handicaps had never been attempted on a broad scale. In the mid-1970s litigation and other pressures successfully challenged the use of standardized test scores as a basis for assigning students to special classes for the retarded. The result was the reassignment of over 11,000 educable mentally retarded (EMR) students to regular classes. Because a disproportionately large number of minority children had been classified as retarded, concerns over the possible violation of their rights had been added to already smoldering doubts concerning the adequacy of educational programs for EMR students.[16]

Under the California Master Plan for Special Education, approved in 1974, California led the nation in integrating students with learning handicaps into regular classes, a policy that became known as "mainstreaming." Whether or not the long-term needs of mentally retarded students are better met in regular or special classes remains to be seen. Nevertheless, by removing the stigma of mental retardation from those who were forced to attend special classes, the new policy did bring some comfort to the families of students who were affected by it.

Mainstreaming received further impetus in California and other states through passage of the Education for All Handicapped Children of Act of 1975, better known among educators as Public Law 94-142. By requiring the placement of children in the "least restrictive" educational environment possible, the legislation furthered the trend of integrating children with physical and mental disabilities into regular classes. Moreover, by requiring the involvement of parents in curriculum planning and preparing individualized instruction programs for every handicapped child, the act might encourage parents of all children to become involved in the educational programs of the schools.

If a real but loosely defined commitment to social justice became the most notable characteristic of the 1960s, the succeeding decade featured the partial and sometimes successful use of specific plans to alleviate injustices. Efforts to equalize the funding for public schools, desegregate the schools, institute programs in bilingual education, and provide for the unique needs of handicapped students represented decisive steps forward.

CHAPTER NINE

A Perspective

Though schools have never been the only educative force in society, they have become the only social institution with education as its primary function. Just as California society has changed dramatically over the past 130 years, so have the character and substance of institutionalized education. The impact of schooling on a society cannot be properly assessed without an understanding of the constraints under which schools operate. The most powerful of those constraints are the values of the dominant culture, for it is that culture that usually controls and finances the schools, administers school programs, and produces most of the teachers. Educational programs have varied over time, but they have not produced—and cannot produce—a society fundamentally different from the one that sponsors them.

Clearly the nation's prevailing economic and political system has done much to define the hopes, realities, and limitations of public schooling. The capitalistic economic order has effectively assured the people that some measure of inequality will prevail from community to community, school to school, family to family, and child to child, but a basic national commitment to the democratic ideal has also assured the people that the more extreme edges of those inequalities would be blunted. California's experience in providing funding for public schools illustrates both the problems and achievements.

Schools are today assumed to be part of society's fabric. Much of the contemporary discussion of public education has focused on inequalities and failings in the system. Schools have fallen short of John Swett's goal of providing a common experience and heritage for the diverse children of the state, educating children for the responsibilities of freedom, insuring universal equality, and guaranteeing prosperity. Inner-city children have rarely been offered an education comparable to that given suburban children, and affluent families almost invariably send their children to better schools than do less fortunate families. Both groups of families are disturbed by the violence, vandalism, and lackluster performance of their children and wonder about the future of public schools.

Though problems abound in education, contemporary reality is still much better than the "good old days" when there was considerable class and racial bias in the schools. Over the years, significant attempts have been made to ameliorate those evils and to strengthen the educational system in other ways. The school year and the number of years of schooling were increased, and schooling was eventually extended to virtually all youngsters, including the poor and the immigrants. The extension of education to every child has led to great emphasis on such practical subjects as woodworking, home economics, sex education, and health.

California's schools, like those in other states, have not only transmitted knowledge and vocational skills to students, but also have influenced the social and moral development of children and youth. This increased responsibility has been accompanied by dramatic growth in the size and cost of the educational enterprise. Within the last decade, federal and state legislation has required the schools to give far greater attention to the educational needs of children with physical, emotional, and learning handicaps. California's children—both normal and handicapped—are now being retained in school longer and being taught by better-educated teachers than at any time in the state's past. If student scores on standardized achievement tests are frequently lower than in previous decades, most of the explanation lies in the greater number and cultural variety of the students taking the tests.

If the schools have sometimes been found wanting, the reasons have as much to do with unrealistic expectations as with program deficiencies. Nearly every major interest group has sought to influence school policy. Since the earliest days of statehood, the privileged classes have expected the school system to secure their property and confirm generally the social and economic status of their children. The poor and aspiring laboring classes, on the other hand, have expected the schools to break down class barriers and produce substantial equality. Perhaps the major achievement of public education during its first century was the difference it made in the lives of white working-class children, not only in their economic success, but also in their expanded knowledge and cultural awareness.

To accommodate such diverse interests the schools had to compromise on major moral and educational questions. Despite such compromises, the schools became California's major instrument for social progress. For the decades ahead the challenge will be to extend to the poor and the nonwhite the social and economic benefits of schooling, while at the same time continuing to serve those classes that historically have been the principal beneficiaries of the system.

In higher education California has rightly achieved a record of greatness in bringing low-cost instruction to almost everyone desiring it. Cost of instruction, however, has raised major questions about the burden, and some citizens wish those benefiting directly from this education to pay a greater part of the expense. The relationship of cost and quality of education has not been resolved after years of argument. In the meantime, officials of state universities face serious problems of budgets and discontented faculties while trying to preserve institutions that have been built over nearly a century of planning. The current financial exigency, nonetheless, has revealed well-constructed universities, with loyal faculties, good facilities, and splendid records of achievement.

Education always will be facing new ideas and crises in a changing society. Fortunately, California's educators have shown a remarkable willingness to meet new challenges with new plans and institutions.

NOTES

CHAPTER TWO

1. John W. Caughey, *California: A Remarkable State's Life History*, 3rd ed. (Englewood Cliffs, N.J.: Prentice-Hall, 1970), 153; Andrew F. Rolle, *California: A History*, 3rd ed. (Arlington Heights, Ill.: AHM Pub., 1978), 172.

2. San Francisco Board of Education, *Annual Report of the Superintendent of Public Schools of the City and County of San Francisco for the Year Ending June 30, 1854* (San Francisco, 1854).

3. John Bigler, "Governor's Special Message to the Senate and Assembly of California, Benicia, Jan. 31, 1854," *Appendix to Assembly Journal* (Sacramento, 1854).

4. Roy W. Cloud, *Education in California* (Stanford, Calif.: Stanford Univ. Press, 1952), 27.

5. California, Superintendent of Public Instruction, *Annual Report of the State Superintendent of Public Instruction, 1858*, in *Appendix to Senate Journal* (Sacramento, 1858), 7.

6. *Annual Report of the State Superintendent* (1858), 14–15.

7. Nicholas C. Polos, *John Swett: California's Frontier Schoolmaster* (Washington, D.C.: University Press of America, 1978), 43.

8. Cloud, *Education in California*, 41.

9. Henry Barnard, "The California Educational Society," *American Journal of Education*, XVI (1866), 789, as quoted in Polos, *John Swett*, 65.

10. California, Superintendent of Public Instruction, *Biennial Report of the State Superintendent of Public Instruction, 1866–1877* in *Appendix to Senate Journal* (Sacramento, 1867), 5.

11. *Calif. Stats.* (1866), c. 342, sec. 56.

12. Cloud, *Education in California*, 46.

CHAPTER THREE

1. William W. Ferrier, *Ninety Years of Education in California* (Berkeley: Sather Gate Book Shop, 1937), 117.

2. Carl B. Swisher, *Motivation and Political Technique in the California Constitutional Convention,* 1878–79 (Claremont, Calif: Pomona College, 1930), 24.

3. Winfield J. Davis, *History of Political Conventions in California, 1849–1892* (Sacramento: California State Library, 1893), 397.

4. *Ward* v. *Flood,* 48 Calif. 36 (1874).

5. Charles M. Wollenberg, *All Deliberate Speed: Segregation and Exclusion in California Schools, 1855–1975* (Berkeley: University of California Press, 1976), 36–38.

CHAPTER FOUR

1. U.S. Bureau of the Census, *Thirteenth Census of the United States,* Vol. II, pt. 1: *Population: Reports by States* (Washington, D.C., 1913), 160, "Table 9: School Attendance."

2. Superintendent Bunker's own story of the junior high school movement in Berkeley is detailed in Frank F. Bunker, *The Junior High School Movement: Its Beginnings* (Washington, D.C.: W. F. Roberts Co., 1935).

3. Resolution of the San Francisco Board of Education, May 5, 1905, as quoted in Arthur G. Butzbach, "The Segregation of Orientals in the San Francisco Schools (M.A. thesis, Stanford University, 1928), 21.

4. The effort of San Francisco officials to segregate Japanese and other Asian students during the early 1900s is detailed in Charles M. Wollenberg, *All Deliberate Speed: Segregation and Exclusion in California Schools, 1855–1975* (Berkeley: University of California Press, 1976), 48–69.

CHAPTER FIVE

1. Otto F. Kraushaar, *Private Schools: From the Puritans to the Present* (Bloomington, Ind.: Phi Delta Kappa, 1976), 28–34.

2. California, Superintendent of Public Instruction, *Biennial Report of the State Superintendent of Public Instruction, 1919–1920* (Sacramento, 1920), 16. The U.S. Census for 1920 reported only 455,000 children, ages 5–14, attending school. Because the data collection methods used by the census bureau and the state superintendent were different, it is impossible to resolve the difference. One is led to conclude,

however, that with a total school attendance figure lower than the claimed public school enrollment, relatively few students could have been attending private schools in 1920.

3. Edward Yeomans, *Shackled Youth* (Boston: Atlantic Monthly Press, 1921).

4. Lorraine M. Sherer, "Curriculum Development in Los Angeles County," California Department of Education, *Bulletin No. 22* (Nov. 1932), 222.

5. *Course of Study for the Kindergarten, First, and Second Grades; Course of Study for the Third and Fourth Grades; Course of Study for the Fifth and Sixth Grades* (Los Angeles City School District, 1924). A more complete description of the progressive education movement in California is found in Irving G. Hendrick, "California's Response to the New Education in the 1930s," *California Historical Quarterly*, LIII (1974), 25–40.

6. Dean Chamberlin *et al., Did They Succeed in College?* (New York: Harper & Bros., 1942), 207–208.

7. "New Methods vs. Old," *Progressive Education*, XVIII (Yearbook Supplement, 1941), 31.

8. San Francisco Board of Education, *Survey of the Elementary Curriculum in San Francisco* (San Francisco: San Francisco Unified School District, 1944), 7.

9. George S. Counts, "Dare Progressive Education Be Progressive," *Progressive Education*, IX (1932), 257–263; and *Dare the Schools Build a New Social Order?* (New York: John Day Co., 1932).

10. "A Review of Public Education in California for the Year 1933," *California Schools*, V (1934), 5.

11. See David Hulburd, *This Happened in Pasadena* (New York: Macmillan, 1951).

12. On October 17, 1952, in the case of *Tolman* v. *Underhill*, 249 P.2d. 280, the California supreme court ruled that the university could not require of its employees "any other oath or declaration relating to loyalty other than that prescribed for all state employees." On the same day the court decided in *Pickman* v. *Leonard*, 249 P.2d.267, that the state's Levering oath was valid.

13. An overview of the university's loyalty oath struggle is found in David P. Gardner, *The California Oath Controversy* (Berkeley: University of California Press, 1967).

CHAPTER SIX

1. *Calif. Stats.* (1889), c. 160, sec. 1776.

2. *Calif. Stats.* (1893), c. 193, sec. 1775.

3. *Mitchell* v. *Winnek,* 117 Calif. 520 (1897).

4. *Calif. Stats.* (1913), c. 695.

5. William F. Eaton, *The American Federation of Teachers, 1916–1961* (Carbondale, Ill.: University of Southern Illinois Press, 1975), 32.

6. "Trends in Salaries," California Teachers Association–Southern Section, *Scope,* X (Oct. 1970), 3.

7. *Calif. Stats.* (1961), c. 848. A detailed account of the political dynamics underlying the Fisher Bill (Senate Bill 57) is found in Irving G. Hendrick, "Academic Revolution in California, A History of Events Leading to the Passage and Implementation of the 1961 Fisher Bill on Teacher Certification," *Southern California Quarterly,* XLIX (1967), 127–166, 253–295, 349–406.

8. The present teacher credentialing policy in California, including establishment of the commission, was approved as Assembly Bill 122, authored by Assemblyman Leo J. Ryan in 1970. In 1978 the commission's composition was modified in favor of more public representatives and fewer higher education representatives through the successful passage of Senate Bill 1051, authored by Senator Arlan Gregorio.

9. Marshall O. Donley, Jr., *Power to the Teacher* (Bloomington, Ind.: Phi Delta Kappa, 1976), 111.

10. Paul Prasow, "Impact of the Rodda Act on California Public Education," in Felicitas Hinman, ed., *Collective Bargaining in California Public Education, S.B. 160—The Rodda Act* (Los Angeles: School of Industrial Relations, University of California, Los Angeles, 1975), 39–40.

CHAPTER SEVEN

1. Verne A. Stadtman, *The University of California, 1868–1968* (New York: McGraw-Hill, 1970), 11.

2. William W. Ferrier, *Ninety Years of Education in California* (Berkeley: Sather Gate Book Shop, 1937), 319.

3. The story of Wheeler's selection and the conditions he set for

accepting the appointment are found in Stadtman, *The University of California*, 181.

4. Clark Kerr, *The Uses of the University* (Cambridge, Mass.: Harvard University Press, 1963).

5. Manuel P. Servín and Iris Higbie Wilson, *Southern California and Its University* (Los Angeles: Ward Ritchie Press, 1969), 269.

6. *Los Angeles Times*, Oct. 16, 1978, pt. 1, p. 20.

7. David Starr Jordan, *The Voice of the Scholar* (San Francisco: P. Elder & Co., 1903), 39.

8. Malcolm G. Scully, "The Well-known Universities Lead in Ratings of Faculties' Reputations," *Chronicle of Higher Education*, XVII (Jan. 15, 1979), 6–7.

9. Shortly after implementation of the Master Plan of Higher Education in California (1960), the individual state colleges were organized as a system. In 1972 the system was officially renamed the California State University and Colleges, with the larger campuses designated as universities and the smaller ones as colleges.

10. See Calif. State Department of Education, Bureau of Junior College General Education, *The Junior College Story* (Sacramento, 1966).

11. Arthur G. Coons, *Crises in California Higher Education* (Los Angeles: Ward Ritchie Press, 1968), 26.

12. Calif. State Department of Education, *A Master Plan for Higher Education in California, 1960–75* (Sacramento: 1960), 73.

13. Guy Benveniste and Charles Benson, *From Mass to Universal Education* (The Hague: Nijhoff, 1976), 68.

14. U.S. Dept. of Health, Education and Welfare, *Digest of Educational Statistics, 1971* (Washington, D.C., 1972), 66.

15. From the 1973 report of the Joint Committee on the Master Plan for Higher Education, as taken from Benveniste and Benson, *From Mass to Universal Education*, 38.

16. Universty of California, Riverside, Office of Budget and Planning, "Fall 1978 Student Ethnicity Comparisons from HEGIS Report XI," Jan. 30, 1979, p. 1.

17. *Regents of the University of California* v. *Bakke*, 438 U.S. 265 (1978).

CHAPTER EIGHT

1. Calif. State Department of Education, *Beyond Serrano: Paying for California's Public Schools* (Sacramento: 1977), 4-5; Calif. State Department of Education, *1975 Report of Enrollment in California's Private Elementary Schools and High Schools* (Sacramento, 1976), 1.

2. Calif. State Department of Education, *1976-77 California Public Schools—Selected Statistics* (Sacramento, 1978), 3.

3. Calif. State Department of Education, *1967-68 California Public Schools—Selected Statistics* (Sacramento, 1969), 1.

4. Don Robinson, "The Conservative Revolution in California Education," *Phi Delta Kappa*, XLII (Dec. 1960), 90.

5. George H. Gallup, "The 10th Annual Gallup Poll of the Public's Attitudes toward the Public Schools," *Phi Delta Kappan*, LX (Sept. 1978), 33-45.

6. See Gerald Kahn and Warren A. Hughes, *Statistics of Local Public School Systems, 1967* (Washington, D.C.: U.S. Office of Education, National Center for Educational Statistics, 1968).

7. A good brief history of California's school finance system prior to 1968 is found in Charles J. Falk, *The Development and Organization of Education in California* (New York: Harcourt, Brace and World, 1968), 107-141.

8. *Serrano* v. *Priest*, 89 Calif. 345 (1971).

9. *Serrano* v. *Priest*, 131 Calif. 228 (1976).

10. *West's Ann. Educ. Code*, Sec. 51212.

11. U.S. Bureau of the Census, *Fourteenth Census, 1920* (Washington, D.C., 1922), Vol. II, pt. 1, pp. 31 and 35.

12. Lawrence B. de Graaf, "The City of Black Angeles: Emergence of the Los Angeles Ghetto, 1890-1930," *Pacific Historical Review*, XXXIX (1970), 330.

13. Calif. Dept. of Education, Bureau of Intergroup Relations, *Racial and Ethnic Distribution in Calif. Public Schools* (Sacramento, 1971), 5.

14. Calif. Dept. of Education, *Enrollment in California's Private Elementary Schools and High Schools* (Sacramento, 1974; 1979).

15. John E. Coons, "Of Family Choice and 'Public' Education," *Phi Delta Kappan*, LXI (Sept. 1979), 10-13; R. Freeman Butts, "Educational Vouchers: The Private Pursuit of the Public Purse," *ibid.*, 7-9.

16. Roland K. Yoshida, Donald L. MacMillan, and C. Edward Meyers, "The Decertification of Minority Group EMR Students in California: Student Achievement and Adjustment," in *Mainstreaming the Minority Child,* edited by Reginald L. Jones (Minneapolis: Council for Exceptional Children, 1976), 215–233.

BIBLIOGRAPHY

MOST SERIOUS SCHOLARSHIP on the history of education has been pursued along topical lines, embracing experiences drawn from the entire nation rather than from a single state. An excellent history of nineteenth- and twentieth-century expansion of public schooling is David B. Tyack, *The One Best System* (Cambridge, Mass.: Harvard University Press, 1974). For a discussion of competing interpretations in the field, consult R. Freeman Butts, "Public Education and Political Community," *History of Education Quarterly*, XIV (1974), 165–183.

General Works

Although no interpretive works have been prepared on the general history of education in California, all of the following contain considerable useful information: Guy Benveniste and Charles Benson, *From Mass to Universal Education: The Experience of the State of Caifornia* (The Hague: Nijhoff, 1976); Roy W. Cloud, *Education in California* (Stanford, Calif.: Stanford University Press, 1952); Charles J. Falk, *The Development and Organization of Education in California* (New York: Harcourt, Brace and World, 1968); William W. Ferrier, *Ninety Years of Education in California, 1846–1936* (Berkeley: Sather Gate Book Shop, 1937); John Swett, *Public Education in California* (New York: American Book Company, 1911).

Specialized Studies

Many sources relating to California education are in the form of unpublished master's theses and doctoral dissertations, with published books and articles being quite sparse. Several biographies have been published on the life and times of California's early superintendents of public instruction. Each presents a contemporary perspective on school conditions and on the state superintendent's relations with members of the legislature and local school officials. Three noteworthy works are David F. Ferris, *Judge Marvin and the Founding of the California Public School System* (Berkeley: University of California Press, 1962); Nicholas C. Polos, *John Swett: California's Frontier Schoolmaster* (Washington, D.C.: University Press of America, 1978); and Solomon P. Jaeckel, "Edward Hyatt, 1858–1919, California Educator," *Southern California Quarterly,* LII (1970), 33–35, 122–154, 248–274.

A valuable description of the early bureaucratic evolution of California's state department of education is contained in Leighton H. Johnson, *Development of the Central State Agency for Public Education in California, 1849–1949* (Albuquerque: University of New Mexico Press, 1952). Parts of California's school finance puzzle are discussed in Arnold J. Meltsner *et al., Political Feasibility of Reform in School Financing: The Case of California* (New York: Praeger, 1973); and Irving G. Hendrick, "The Impact of the Great Depression on Public School Support in California," *Southern California Quarterly,* LIV (1972), 177–195.

Precious few historical studies have been written on curriculum in the state. Two articles by Irving G. Hendrick discuss parts of that story: "The Early History of California State-Printed Textbooks," *Southern California Quarterly,* LII (1974); and "California's Response to the 'New Education' in the 1930s," *California Historical Quarterly,* LII (1974), 25–40. Most material relating to teacher education and certification in California remains in unpublished dissertations. One exception is Irving G. Hendrick, "Academic Revolution in California: A History of Events Leading to the Passage and Implementation of the 1961 Fisher Bill on Teacher Certification," *Southern California Quarterly,* XLIX (1967), 127–166, 253–295, 359–406.

The history of educating California's minority citizens represents one of the most prolific areas of scholarship. Special attention should be given to Charles M. Wollenberg, *All Deliberate Speed: Segregation and Exclusion in California Schools, 1855–1975* (Berkeley: University of California Press, 1976); and Irving G. Hendrick, *The Education of Nonwhites in California, 1849–1970* (San Francisco: R. and E. Research Associates, 1977).

Institutional histories, too numerous to list, are available on many of California's older colleges and universities. David P. Gardner's *The California Oath Controversy* (Berkeley: University of California Press, 1967) provides valuable insight into how the public's fear of communism during the late 1940s and early 1950s affected higher education. Two worthwhile sources concerning the planning difficulties faced by the state's higher education system are California State Department of Education, *A Master Plan for Higher Education in California, 1960-1975* (Sacramento, 1960); and Arthur G. Coons, *Crises in California Higher Education* (Los Angeles: Ward Ritchie Press, 1968).

Commentaries on contemporary problems facing education in California have been published in numerous places. See especially the September, 1978, issue of the *Phi Delta Kappan* (Vol. 60), which contains the following: Joan C. Baratz and Jay H. Moskowitz, "Proposition 13: How and Why It Happened," 9-11; James W. Guthrie, "Proposition 13 and the Future of California's Schools," 12-15; and William R. Hazard, "The *Bakke* Decision: Mixed Signals from the Court," 16-19. While the Gallup Poll's findings are not restricted to California, important insights into the strengths and ills of contemporary education in California and elsewhere can be found in George H. Gallup, "The 10th Annual Gallup Poll of the Public's Attitudes toward the Public Schools," *Phi Delta Kappan*, LX (1978), 33-45.

INDEX